GOING HOME:
A BACKPACKER'S JOURNEY

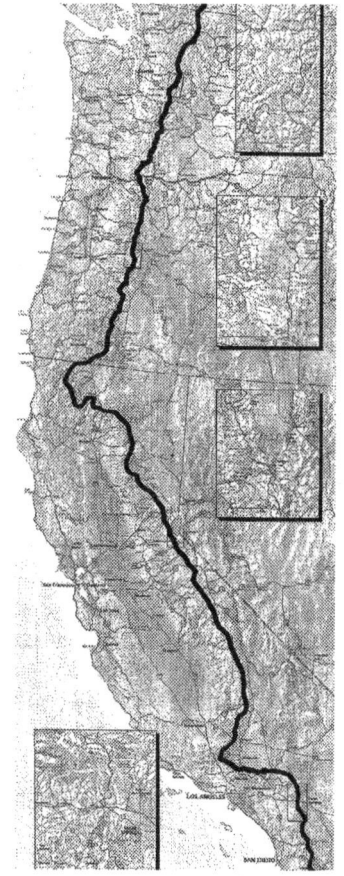

by Thomas Ashley Young

Copyright © 2007 by Thomas Ashley Young

Going Home
A Backpacker's Journey
by Thomas Ashley Young

Printed in the United States of America

ISBN 978-1-60266-362-6

All rights reserved solely by the author. The author guarantees all contents are original and do not infringe upon the legal rights of any other person or work. No part of this book may be reproduced in any form without the permission of the author. The views expressed in this book are not necessarily those of the publisher.

Unless otherwise indicated, Bible quotations are taken from the King James version of the Bible. Copyright © 1999 by Holman Bible Publishers.

www.xulonpress.com

PRELUDE

Consider placing half your body weight in a knapsack. Now strap this load to your back. Begin to walk on uneven ground. Imagine further a foul weather day in the midst of all this. Finally, after taking 500 steps, stop.

You have just covered three-tenths of a mile on a simulated segment of the Pacific Crest Trail (or PCT). You now have exactly two thousand, four hundred fifty two miles left to hike, even though you don't know this at the time. All you know is the "trail" which is immediately in front of you. At times you will count the seconds, one by one. By the time you finish hiking, nearly fifteen million seconds will have elapsed.

This was my journey in 1981.

In this particular account, all seconds and tenths-of-a-mile have not been depicted, even though the surrounding details are accurate. (To "paint" the entire hike would mean a book longer than the trail itself!) Yet for the most part, after all those millions of seconds, I found on the easel of trail-dust: not a trail-long book, but rather a painting depicting the corridors of my own soul. What an unveiling shock this was!

Picture yourself as that one, for a moment. We all find ourselves alone: even in a crowd, at one time or another. In fact, as we read any book, it is nearly impossible not to be alone. Indeed, when all is said and done, we all must face solitude by coming to grips with the individual we see when we look in the mirror. And furthermore, we must all deal with everyday things that tend to ricochet off that mirror, down into the depths of our own souls. This we must all do, while in turn hiking within the confines of our own daily pathway.

I have nicknamed those I met along the way. Look within these ones: their natures, their hearts, their souls. Perhaps you will see yourself in one or more of them.

Even though I hiked this entire 2,452.3-mile-long footpath solo, there were others who walked the entire trail that same year. One in particular, who walked well in front of me, revealed himself only after trail's end. Long after the hike was over, as we met and discussed the trail, I came to realize that he was the only one who truly understood my journey, with all of its emotional upheavals. If a dedication in this book is to be made, it is to him (you will find out later who he is).

One point of note here: The year after the hike, I "knew" I was going to write a book about the PCT. The year after that, I knew I would NOT write a book about the PCT. Thus, I threw all my journals away! But decades later, my dedicated friend came on board to help me write.

This book is the result.

So come along with me on this trail. I am certain you will see things that you have never seen before.

INTRODUCTION

"But you don't even know how to camp!"
"You're too skinny to carry such a load!"
"The bears will eat you alive!"

When I was growing up, I went to Sunday school every week. Enroute to the classroom one Sunday morning, I had asked, "Who are these 12 husky fishermen in nice frames on the wall here?" To which came the reply, "They fished with Jesus."

On Saturdays, I tried to be a fisherman - a 'man of the outdoors' - as my dad took me to a lake: the same one, every time. Rattigan Lake: that's what its name was, near my hometown of Grand Rapids, Michigan. My dad would always push a few dollar bills into the old wooden box by the unlocked rowboats to pay for the rental, and then we would push off from the lily pad-lined lakeshore. Once reaching the middle of the lake, we would drop anchor, and begin to fish. Our boat was the only one on the lake just about every time we went out. It was always very quiet in the rowboat, as we waited in the middle of the lake, yet also very boring for an eight-year-old who did not know how to fish. Dad had tried to teach me all about the knots: i.e., how to tie the fish lines and all, when he wasn't busy staring at the water, puffing on his pipe, trying to coax a fish by the flicking of his fishing rod... but I just couldn't seem to catch on. In other words, I had tried, like 12 husky others, to be a good fishing buddy for my dad, but I was never able to learn the knots that well.

I kept attending Boy Scouts without a father figure.

My first big project while scouting was to construct a pack frame from scratch. The opportunity to test it out came during a weekend jaunt along the Grand River. I can still recall the fresh smell of varnish emanating from my pack frame as I quickly attached the burlap sack and my bedroll to it, at the start of the hike. The air was fresh and crisp that morning, and our troup started out in single file. Yet only a few hundred yards into the hike, my sleeping bag came loose from my pack frame *(my knots...! now unraveling!)*, and proceeded to tumble down a steep slope toward the river. My face turned beet-red as I descended the hill amidst trail-side laughter to retrieve my bedroll. To this day, I still do not know how two small birch trees suddenly appeared to stop my rolling parcel from becoming a statistic at the bottom of the river. Perhaps it was the God of the husky fishermen I was told, but at the time I was simply embarrassed.

Boy Scouts faded, and college sprouted - into the knotty maze of 'higher education.' Near the end of my tenure, when asked about my areas of interest by the on-site career counselor, my only response was that I had not the foggiest idea of what there was to be interested in.

So, to escape all the non-interests, I loaded up my old Dodge, and began to drive west. The boring Rattigan Lake syndrome came rushing back into my mind as I drove the many miles of corn fields that grew along Highway 80. But after reaching the Rocky Mountains, my heart became captivated by the heights, even beyond any ridiculing voices that echoed '...you are not to be a man of the outdoors ...'

Thus, the long-distance seed of my upcoming walk was born.

Faith sometimes has funny friends.

CHAPTER 1:
THE TRAIL ITSELF

"Name?" the Resident Ranger (RR) asked me, from behind a map-strewn desk.

"Yes, I have one…"

RR looked at me strangely. "I beg your pardon?"

"Huh? Oh, sorry. My name's Ashley," I said, looking around the room.

A pause. "And I suppose your girlfriend's name is Scarlet O'Hara," came the terse reply.

'I wish you were gone with the wind,' I muttered, under my breath.

The ranger shot an unsuspecting narrow glance at me. "Now listen, sir, we need to have this information in order to monitor the number of people in the wilderness properly. So may I have your name, please?"

The procedure seemed to take forever. Here I was, enroute to my first dayhike in the mountains not far northeast of San Diego, encountering an unlikely obstacle. With awkwardness (after the ranger finally accepted my middle name), I unfolded the booklet-sized map that was in the 'free handout' section of the rack near the door, and pretended to look it over closely. When I looked up, RR was still penning something on my permit form.

"What's this PCT?" I asked, pointing to one trail-segment.

RR's face changed. "Oh, that's the Pacific Crest Trail," he chimed. "It splits the San Jacinto mountain range through this area in a north-south direction. The whole trail is really something else."

"Sounds good. How long is it? I'd like to hike it."

RR slowly put down his pen, his expression having changed back to tightness. "It would take you six months to hike it. Our wilderness area contains only a small portion of it. It goes all the way to Mexico, 200 miles to the south."

I stopped. "Huh?"

RR smiled at my expression. "Well," he laughed, "that's nothing! Because if you follow it 2,000 miles to the north, you'll run into Canada!"

I could only stare, eyes wide.

"Of course, you can just hike sections of it," he went on to say. "I've always dreamed of doing the whole thing. But that takes planning, considering everything involved."

"You must be kidding about all of this!" I shot back. "I've never heard of such a long trail. Who in his right mind would ever attempt it?" I asked.

He paused. "Anyone with time, money and determination, I suppose."

"Do you have a map of the whole trail?"

RR laughed. "No, but here's where you can get one." He scribbled down the address of a publishing company, somewhere in central California.

"Thanks. Thanks very much." I headed for the door.

"Don't forget your permit," he said, waving it in the air after me.

"Oh, sorry. I almost forgot. Can you change it to include the whole trail?"

RR gave me another strange look. Then cocking his head, he exclaimed, "Why you – you impulsive greenfoot! Don't you think you'd better do some research, and think it over?!"

Going Home

I cowered. "Yeah, well, probably. Sorry, I just got excited. I'll take the day pass for now."

30 minutes later at the trailhead parking lot, I pulled out my gear. It took about 5 minutes of rustling through the car to get my backpack, and then *another* 15 minutes for the backpack to be hoisted and positioned properly on my back. I was so excited that I had to return to the car three times to see if I had forgotten anything.

Now on the trail, I imagined myself walking thousands of miles. It felt good. I let out a big "WHOOP!" and a smile. Each trail section went well, and I relished the breeze.

But a couple hours later, I encountered my first "saddle" on an open plateau, and slowly took off my backpack to investigate the 'trail convergence' a bit more closely. There were many signs nailed on many trees. I looked at the map, but footnotes were nowhere to be found. I may as well have been on the moon trying to decipher which trail led in which direction! After yelling at one of the signs, I started to tromp in all directions. It took a long time before I located a tree with a shiny metal object nailed to it. A PCT trail-emblem stared me in the face. And I stared back at it.

Behind the tree was Canada. Behind me was Mexico.

It was time to head home and plan.

CHAPTER 2:
RESEARCH AND READINESS

Summertime 1980: vacation time! For everyone else.
In the span of June, July and August, I wrote to anyone even remotely associated with this thing called the Pacific Crest Trail (PCT). As a result, I wore out countless typewriter ribbons, and basically eliminated myself from the social realm of life. Long before summer's end, my friends were wondering what had happened to me, and sent one of them bursting through my apartment-door.

The noise of the door hitting the wall startled me. I turned to look, but before I could answer, Maps Man (nearly out of breath) exclaimed, "He - hey Ash, thu - there's a good (he paused to catch his breath) flick on tonight on the tube. Afterward we can go and tip a few. Wha'cha say?" (Maps Man, or "Sport" for short, had obtained all the necessary trail maps free of charge, and then had 'sported' them off to me as if they were Chamber of Commerce brochures.)

"Can't do it, Sport. I've got planning to do."

There was a pause, but not for breath. "But you do that every day! Don't you think you need a break?"

"I don't have time. Besides, I would be thinking of the trail at the bar. This thing is really important to me, and I don't want to blow it."

My friend suddenly wrinkled his brow, in an attempt to understand. "Yeah, sounds like quite a trip. How long is this thing?"

"About 2,500 miles or so. The way I figure it, I might just make it in about three years."

Maps Man looked at me strangely. "You - you mean, without stopping?"

I smiled.

"But what about the weather?" he asked. "Wouldn't you have to quit during the winter?"

I paused. "Hmmm. I see what you mean. I may be checking back with you."

Maps Man headed for the door, leaving me to my knotty maze.

Ah yes, the weather. Snows don't start to melt in the southernmost mountains until well into April, and then they 'reappear' in the northernmost ones by October. And in-between would probably be year-round snow. *How am I ever going to tackle this?*

***

In the fall and winter months that followed, I actively studied other mazes such as bulk foods and expedition equipment. As a result, I became firmly entrenched in my own little bundle of insanity. For example, while in the supermarket one day, I completely emptied a shelf-section of Ramen noodles, canned tuna fish, and orange-flavored drink powder while patrolling the floor for specials. In the checkout line, an old lady eyed me suspiciously.

"The - the store's going to be here tomorrow, sonny," she said, nervously.

I looked at my overflowing cart and then at her. "Well yes, Ma'am, but I may not be!" I then turned to the checkout clerk, who was trying to remain calm.

Going Home

Things started piling high in my bedroom. Places to store my carloads of preserved food were becoming scarce. Maps Man didn't have much storage space, either. Perhaps I could store it with Pro Verbs, up north?

Pro Verbs was a lady I had met soon after moving to San Diego. In the end, she opted to travel to Alaska to work for the summer, but we always stayed in touch. Perhaps, just perhaps, she could mail the dried food to me marked "General Delivery – Hold For PCT Hiker", as I walked from south to north, at scheduled intervals. The cost factor would of course be astronomical, but she had proven herself more than dependable to me.

"Hello?"

I paused. "So how's Alaska?" I asked.

Another pause. "So how's the trip planning?" came the reply.

A third pause. "Well, let me tell you..."

By late January and early February of 1981, I was working frantically to solve all the final pre-trek details. A couple weeks later, the Post Office began to see me regularly, as I mailed off parcel after parcel to Alaska. Some of the food items I mailed included bags of Granola/Powdered Milk (for breakfast), juice crystals (to kill the iodine taste of purified stream or lake water), tubes of peanut butter (for lunch), meatless pemmican and GORP (for snacks), ramen noodles and tuna (for dinner), powdered cheesecake (for desert), and powdered cocoa (for an evening hot drink). I was hoping to catch some huckleberries and fish along the way, but at best these 'food items' would be supplemental.

My backpack was a custom-made internal frame gem, and would be my "house" for nearly six months. It was certainly much better than the Boy Scout one I had constructed years ago! I would carry within its confines almost half my body weight in food, clothing, tent, map/compass, knife, small stove and fuel, and other small items that had been stripped of unnecessary weight.

The preparations had been intense.

In March, the schedule was finalized that Pro Verbs would use to send me the parcels from an Alaskan Post Office (each containing about one week's worth of supplies). It became clear to me that I would need to receive over 20 such parcels during the course of the journey just in order to survive. The financial strain proved at times to be overwhelming. I was thankful for my job at a nearby camping and surplus store: for the availability of needed items near cost, and for the stability of conversing with others each day in language that related to the hike.

Whenever exercising, I did not play the part of a San Diego resident. In other words, a person walking along the beach on a very hot day is clearly out of place if he wears wool socks, hiking boots, and a backpack. It was on one of my outings that I distinctly remembered being startled by a booming voice.

"Hey! Wha'cha doin'?!"

I turned to see a man on a blanket in the sand. It was instantly obvious to me that he was not in training.

"I'm breakin' in my boots," I said.

"But why HERE?" he asked.

I stopped to look at the man. "Why NOT here?" I countered.

He took a sip of his drink. "Well," he continued, "they make trails somewhere else, you know."

I continued hiking.

In early March, about a month before the planned start of my hike, I opened the door of a familiar office. A surprised look met me from behind the map-strewn desk.

Surprise gave way to laughter. "I remember," RR, the Resident Ranger began, "when you first came in here. You were pretty wet behind the ears then."

"I believe you used the term 'greenfoot,'" I said.

He laughed again. "So what brings you back to this neck of the woods in winter?"

"In winter?" *Maps Man had mentioned this to me in San Diego quite a while back, but...*

"Winter lasts well into April in these parts," RR continued. "Snows still obliterate the trail at the higher elevations. You would have to trudge, as it were, cross-country. You *did* prepare for this type of thing, didn't you?"

Strangely enough, I had not even considered the extent of the snow coverage. Training on San Diego beaches had revealed not even one snowflake.

"But you'll be alone up there, that's for sure!" he added.

"I'd still like a permit."

"Yeah, OK. For how long?"

"A couple of weeks."

A blank look entitled "*HOW long?*" stared back at me.

By the time I had reached the same saddle of the previous year, I was knee-deep in snow. Fear began to sweep over me, as my mind began a sort of negative cadence of its own. *What happens if I DON'T find a suitable campsite? And when I DO stop to camp, won't it get too cold? And you've never built a fire before! Also, what about ...*

"Ash, you're back!"

Maps Man had just barged through my apartment door, as was his custom. A jumbled mass of wet, dirty equipment lay on the living room floor, and I was in the midst of it.

"Yeah, I made it," I muttered.

"Wow, you look beat. Was it that hard?"

I sighed. "There's a cold beer in the fridge, if you want it."

"But what about - "

"Sit down," I interjected.

My friend took the chair nearest to me. I looked up at him from the floor.

"There's way too much snow up there," I began. "In another two weeks I'm planning to take off for real, and soon after that I'll hit the same area again. It took forever for me to hike through it all!"

Maps Man look at me for what seemed like a very long time. Then, wrinkling his brow, he said, "I think I'll get that beer." Upon his return to the living room, he asked me (in the middle of a gulp), "Well, hey, don't you think some of it might melt before then?"

"Well yeah, I tried to remind myself of that, but my mind was tripping out on too many things. I guess - I guess snow-walking and me just don't get along too well."

The next day at work, I was pulled aside.

"You're leaving next week, right?" I was asked.

I was in the middle of stocking boots in an aisle of the camping and surplus store. "That's right," I replied.

"Well, why is it that you can't hunt or fish for your food along the way? Seems to me that would be easier than having it all mailed."

"Takes too long," I said, adding a size 10 pair of boots to the aisle. "I have to make an average of 17 miles per day, every day, for the whole six month duration. But," I added, "there'll be berry and fish supplements, and pit stops at town stores. Ice cream will taste soOOO good!"

"Can I go with you?"

"Huh?" I exclaimed, knocking some boots off the shelf.

"I mean, you'll need a partner, won't you?" he continued.

Oh, great, I thought. *I already tried that with my Assistant Manager, planning as a two-some. All he wanted to do was party ...*

I stood up, not quite looking at him. "Well, uh listen - I, um - this takes a lot of planning, and I'm due to leave soon. You wouldn't be ready for this type of thing."

"Sure I would!" he shot back.

"You mean you have the vision?" I asked.

"The what?"

"You know, the vision. That which gets you through the hard spots."

He stopped, putting his hands in his pockets.

"Well, I can handle it, you know!" he finally said.

I turned to face him squarely. His teenage-type response would need a more detailed reply.

"Could you? I mean, are you able to carry three weeks worth of food in a 60 pound pack, through mountains and snow?"

He backed up. "Uhhh..."

"Or are you able to handle the 15 miles a day of desert hiking?"

"Er - um - I - I'm not sure," he skittishly replied.

I grabbed his shoulder. "Well, you'd better be! Look, I don't mean to be rough, but you'd better count the cost before you even think about hiking this thing!"

"You sound like my mother," he said.

That stopped me. "What?"

"My Mom. She was always speaking to me from the Bible. And I specifically remember her talking about some counting-the-cost thing in regards to my coming to San Diego in the first place."

"The Bible? Wha - ? Man, I haven't looked at one of those things in years! And besides, I'm not your mother! I'm just - "

"Aren't you going to take one?" he interrupted.

"Take what?" I asked.

"A Bible. You'll need God's help for this hike, won't you?"

"Huh?"

"And what about the bears?" he continued.

I paused, thinking about the Bible. "Oh, they'll not be a problem. The trailguide speaks of very few bears, seeing

Going Home

as how the PCT goes through some very heavily traveled areas."

"But son, what about the bears?"

I had just called my Mom to tell her all things were going well into my final week before takeoff. I had not, but should have, anticipated this type of question.

"The what, Mom?"

"Do you have a gun?" I thought she asked next.

"It weighs too much, Mom. I've got firecrackers instead."

There was a long silence.

"Mom, look," I continued. "I really appreciate your support. I know you don't really understand why I'm doing this, but - "

"Good luck, son."

Pro Verbs sounded nervous over the phone.

"I'm over-budget, Ash, but I believe in you."

"Thanks," I said. "Just think of this as an adventure you're sharing in," I added.

"I am. I mean, I'm really trying to. But being knee-deep in granola and some other things you sent, it kind of spoils the effect."

I had to laugh.

"But I'm trying to stay ahead of the hiking schedule you mailed me, by sending out these first two parcels, ... and you haven't even started yet!"

"Tomorrow," I stated. "I'll keep in touch when I can."

CHAPTER 3:
THE START FRIDAY,
APRIL 10, 1981:
MILE ZERO

I was ready to go, I thought. Unfortunately, on the takeoff day, my backpack weighed in at a mind-boggling 76 pounds. Wild Bill, the only person I knew who had a rig big enough to carry my load, lifted it with the greatest of difficulty.

"For crying out loud, Ash, you're going to hike HOW far with this thing?!"

"You don't understand," I replied. "I'm at a bare minimum now." I turned to look at the pack, again, which filled the back seat. "But I have to admit I *am* afraid of the size of it."

A pause. "Just be sure you need it all."

"Yeah, OK. Let's get going. I'll try to cut out some weight along the way."

The ride to the Mexican border from San Diego was a very long one. "My arm hurts, Ash, from lifting your backpack," Wild Bill began, as we hit the freeway. "But it's great to be on the road!"

I glanced over at him, saying nothing. My thoughts were not so much centered on the scenery passing by or upon his statements, but rather on what scenery would lie ahead on the 24" wide footpath. *Can I really pull this thing off?* I began to muse. *Do I really know what I am doing?*

Going Home

On and on we traveled, it seemed. The sun was hot as we exited the highway onto paved back roads. Pavement then gave way to dirt.

Wild Bill had started to hum as a certain song came over the radio. "Yee-haw!" he guffawed, as his VW Bus swathed through a row of low-hanging tree branches. "Best vacation day I ever took!"

I smiled, but not really.

"Ash, I think we're here."

I looked up. I had been so consumed with my thoughts that I had neglected to spot the road for Wild Bill. In front of the VW Bus was a barbed-wire fence.

"Ash?" he asked, a bit subdued.

I shook myself. "Well," I finally began, "I know the temporary trail starts on a road, in front of a fence like this."

"What do you mean," he retorted, "you've never been here before?!"

"It's in the guidebook, WB. The first few miles of trail are on a dirt road like this since they haven't completed the permanent PCT through this area."

Wild Bill frowned. "Give me a break, man! What is this, state politics or something?"

I laughed. "Maybe," I quipped, looking back at the fence.

"So where's the sign?" Wild Bill finally asked.

He meant the PCT sign. "Haven't the foggiest," I said, after a pause.

"Well, I saw a fork in the road a bit further back. Wanna try it?"

I looked again at the fence. "Yeah, yeah. Let's get going," I said.

We finally came to another barbed-wire fence, after zig-zagging through a long stretch in the dirt road. My friend got out of the vehicle to read the fairly large sign on one of the fence-posts. "Pa - ci - ic Cr - st... Ash, you'd better come look at this," I heard him say.

I slowly got out of the VW Bus, walked over to the sign, and squinted. "Yep, this is it," I said. "Just a little worn, that's all."

"Hmmm...," was all my friend could say.

We both looked around, and then at each other. "So this is it?" Wild Bill asked, after what seemed like an interminable silence.

I stared past him, and asked, "So where's the band, the dramatic sendoff?"

"I'M your dramatic sendoff, Ash. Give me your camera and I'll take a few photos of you at the start here. You DO have a camera somewhere in that elephant-sized pack of yours, don't you?"

Click, click, click. I didn't remember the sequence. I could only look north, over Wild Bill's shoulder. For the next six months, I would be mailing back undeveloped rolls of film so that others could live my trek in delayed mode. I would see none of the shots until after I finished.

"I took three pictures. Is that enough?" he asked, handing the camera back to me.

"Fine. Yeah, just fine."

He paused. "I just hope you meet some people. Things could get pretty lonely out in a place like this."

I nodded. The country Wild Bill was referring to was the desert-like terrain that surrounded us as far as the eye could see. It was laced with knee-high Manzanita shrubs and small brush-like trees.

"I'll call you or Maps Man collect at my first stop," I said.

Wild Bill slapped my shoulder. "OK." And with that, he climbed back into his bus and sped off. The sound of the engine shifting through the gears faded away after only a few seconds, and I was left alone.

Going Home

I turned to face the fence. Someone had left a notebook there. I then added my name to the five others who were hiking a few days ahead of me. Then I sat down on the ground, and leaned into my 76 pound "home". It was certainly no Boy Scout rucksack, that's for sure. I placed my arms into the straps, and then rolled over on my side to push up to my knees. Using my ice axe as a staff, I then stood upright, wobbling just a bit. It took only a few minutes to cinch all the backpack straps in place. I carefully placed one foot underneath the fence marking the start of the PCT after a few moments, and exclaimed "Mexico!"

And then I headed north.

CHAPTER 4:
ON THE ROAD FRIDAY, APRIL 17, 1981; MILE 114.0 AT ANZA, CALIFORNIA

I trudged slowly up the road, my mind in surrealistic thought. I had been hiking for only a few minutes, when I heard "Hey, meeEEEster!"

I looked over to my right. *Wha - ?* I wondered, startled.

"You sneak over de border?" the man asked.

I squinted at him. "No. No, I'm just hiking!"

"Ho-kay."

Thus, my 'start' from the Mexican border was now complete.

Gradually, over the course of the next few days, I developed a workable routine. Awake when first daylight appears, pack everything in-between eating breakfast (which usually consisted of granola soaked in water and powdered milk), and then be off before sunrise. Check maps at each break (usually once an hour), replenishing body with quick-energy food and liquids. Take a few photos for effect. Stop for a one-hour lunch near mid-day. Remonstrate the hips, knees and feet when they complain. Watch the path of the sun starting mid-afternoon, and time the daily stop near a water source just before the sun goes down. Set up camp. Then eat dinner, relax, and ponder different orientation of items in backpack, and/or elimination of certain items when able to properly dispose of them. Compile a list of things to mail back to Alaska when reaching the 'Post Office Resupply Point.' Journal thoughts.

And here I was on this, my seventh day hiking, walking into the town of Anza, California, with over one hundred miles behind me and over twenty three hundred to go. It was only just yesterday that a new section of trail had dead-ended into 10-foot high chaparral, making the push to get to the temporary (dirt road) 'trail' a very scratchy experience. And I had yet to contend with the hottest desert and the coldest mountains stretches.

"May I help you?" quipped an old lady from behind the counter.

"Yes, you may. I should have a package labeled 'HOLD FOR PCT HIKER' here."

She cocked her head to look more closely at me, and then wrote something on a nearby pad of paper. "I'll need to see some ID, please," she finally said.

I unzipped the top pouch of my backpack, and pulled out a baggie stuffed with map-sections and assorted other paperwork. I pulled out the little plastic card and handed it to her.

She looked at my driver's license, and then at me. "You look a little different from the photo," she blankly stated.

"Trail dust," I replied.

"Hmmm. Well, let's see here," she said, ignoring the comment, "looks like you have three boxes."

"Three?"

She smiled. "And you can sign this if you want to."

I wrinkled my brow. "Why?"

"It's the Pacific Crest Trail register. All hikers passing through usually sign it."

I applied pen to paper, and noted a few other names that had been signed only a day or two previously. I made a mental note of them.

It took a while to open the first and largest box, and then to organize its contents in my pack. It had certainly come a

Going Home

long way, through many Alaska and California label markings. The second box (from Mom) I consumed instantly (chocolate chip cookies were its lot), and the third was simply a note wrapped in newspaper from San Diego: "Thought you'd like to see some civilization in this wrapping, Ash. Call me collect if you need anything. Signed, Maps Man."

Before going to the phone, however, I sat down to write some letters. What flowed first was the start of a poem to Pro Verbs: my main supply source, to the north:

I love the things you did within
The box you sent so well
And though I only see the food
I know you went through hell:
To pack the box: so patiently;
To compose within: variety;
It will keep me going, in spite of me,
And -

I stopped. *Maybe it's better to call Maps Man before I mail this...*

"Collect call from Ashley Pacemaker. Will you accept charges?"

"Hey, wow, WILL I? Yeah, put him on!"

"Go ahead."

"Ash! You made it! Are you OK? Where are you? Is everything all right? And - "

"Whoa, WHOA, sport. Slow down. Yes, yes, I'm fine. Just trying to deal with my feet, and the lack of trail water, that's all."

"So how is - the trail? I mean, are you still – going to keep hiking?"

"Sure," I said. "But hey, listen to this." I read him the start of the piece I had just composed, to send up north.

There was a long pause at the end of the line.

"Sounds pretty weird to me, Ash. I can't stand poetry."

"Well, I didn't write it for you."

Another pause. "OK, just don't print it with my name on it, alright?"

I laughed. "You still going to meet me up the line?"

"Of course! Just like we planned."

"OK."

There was one pizza shop in town. Three other "through-hikers" were already there, in process of having a feast for thirty. They motioned for me to pull up a chair, and I sat down.

"We started about ten days ago," Laid Back Louie started, "and we took it slow. Had to catch a few sights, you know!"

"Yeah, right!" Appalachian Trailheader added. "And now that we're here, it's time to forget the back roads. Man, at least the AT (or Appalachian Trail, which ran nearly the same distance as the PCT, from Georgia to Maine) didn't have roads to hike."

I looked at the third hiker, who had consumed nearly three pizzas. Chow Down offered me a large slice, laced with pineapple and beef, and I took a bite. *My*, I thought, *this food sure beats that dried stuff...*

"So what's YOUR biggest obstacle thus far, Ash?" AT asked me.

I pondered thoughtfully, in-between a large mouthful of cheese and crust. "Well, this dog, you see," I began, wiping my mouth with the back of my hand, "nearly scared me out of my wits this shmornin'." (I swallowed) "I was sleeping soundly in the park: you know, that one on the south end of town? Well, the next thing I know there's this barking only two inches from one of my ears. Man, it scared the living daylights out of me." As if on cue, the whole table erupted in laughter.

"But get this," I continued, "I fell back asleep again after he scurried away, and then he did it again!" AT started clapping his hands, as Laid Back Louie leaned back in his chair almost too far.

Six eyes then told me to continue my story.

"Well, he was too quick," I went on. "Anyway, the *third* time, I pretended to fall back asleep, keeping my sleeping bag unzipped. Out of the corner of my eye I watched him slowly zigzag back through the park toward me. When he got about ten yards away, I jumped out of my bag in a full sprint toward him, barking at the top of my lungs. Man, you never saw a dog move so fast!"

"So THAT'S why you got sore feet!" Chow Down interjected, slapping his leg a couple of times with a palm-full of cheese.

We had all camped in a vacant lot just on the east outskirts of town. My three friends had erected their massive tent, but I opted to sleep out under the stars.

I awoke with the sun the next morning. Nearby, the other three hikers were fast asleep. I turned on my pocket flashlight to take a look at the map. The high country was just ahead.

I decided to skip my Anza layover. Maybe it was the excitement of the ongoing hike, or maybe it was the "need" for hiking solitude. Regardless, I packed in less than thirty minutes, and was off.

The first few miles hiking were along a winding stretch of highway. Thunk, thunk, thunk, went the methodical stomping of my boots against the pavement, and then shunk, shunk, shunk, as I shifted my feet to the more-padded gravel shoulder. Thunk, thunk, thunk; shunk, shunk, shunk; thunk, shunk, thunk, shunk... The cadence was to become part of my hiking routine. Eventually in the distance, I could see the takeoff point of "real trail." Upon reaching it, I noted a sign and grinned.

It was a very real non-road portion of the PCT, and those first few steps on it were extremely liberating.

Now meandering through desert-like Manzanita and chaparral brush, I stopped every so often to admire the silence. By early afternoon, I had gained notable elevation. With my white-gas stove the size of a softball, I melted some of the snow from an isolated snow-bank to make water, as streams, rivers and springs were non-existent.

By mid-afternoon, I had gained wind-swept ridgelines. This was my first taste of the high country, and I relished the breeze once again.

The San Jacinto mountain range was my first formidable barrier along the PCT. The trail snaked up toward and around 8,800-foot-high Taquitz (Tah-KEETS) Peak, before heading through the saddle I had come upon in my pre-trek training. I had multitudes of conflicting thoughts flowing through my head as I wound my way through an area burned by fire and covered by snow just a few trail-miles south of the peak. I had unfortunately underestimated the mileage to my next potential campsite: twilight began closing in as the PCT continued to hug the slopes of Taquitz. I ended up having to camp right on the trail itself as darkness enfolded me. Once again, melted snow formed the basis for my water supply.

The next day, I crawled outside my bag to greet the morning chill, and packed. Before long, I began hiking, wiggling my toes as I went, trying to work the cold out of my boots. My breath stayed visible a good part of the first hour. The trail came up over a small ridge, and opened up on a plateau ... to a field of knee-deep snow.

The trail was nowhere in sight.

Suddenly, I heard a voice from behind. "Where *am* I?!" I turned to see Appalachian Trailheader, alias AT, stumble frantically across the white terrain toward me. I tightened my pack as he came closer, and it became obvious to me that he wanted to get out of the snowfield - now. I tried to answer him as he passed by, but was interrupted by "I (puff puff) I - never met anything like *this* on the AT!" In short order though, he faded into the distance, and the silence returned.

I stooped down to retrieve some snowmelt.

The end of the snow pack did come, but not until I had slugged through knee-deep snow for the better part of an hour. The extra effort was truly exhausting. My body became soaked below the knees. After what seemed like days, the exposed trail finally appeared in an open field laced with boulders. I stopped, bending over to catch my breath in long drawn-out gulps. As I straightened, my eyes became captivated by the sun shining in its strength from the deep-blue sky. Ice-sheathed shrubbery glistened on the ridgeline above. It was truly a sight to behold.

As I came around the flanks of 10,000-foot-high Mount San Jacinto, I sat down on an exposed rock. An energy bar was quickly consumed. I slowly stood and began to resume my more-or-less northward course. Up and over a ridge the trail went, and then down, down, down in switchback patterns to the valley below, which was covered with pine trees. The PCT finally leveled out near a dirt road crossing, at a sign:

"BEYOND THIS POINT, TRAIL IS DIFFICULT TO FIND"

I remembered reading about this section in the guidebook, not wanting to believe it. The reason for the difficulty, the guidebook said, was that brush fires in previous seasons had fertilized the soil with nitrogen-rich nutrients, which in turn would feed new prickly chaparral growth, which in turn would (in time) completely obliterate the trail.

"One should take the designated alternate route: the dirt road, around the area of the burn," the guidebook went on to say. I cringed, wondering at the sanity of the writer. "Around the area?" I asked out loud. "But just how hard can it *be* to hike a mere two miles cross-country?!"

* * * * * *

Three hours later, scratched and marred by the desert-like, eight-foot-high brush that overwhelmed the hillside, I entered upon Hurley Flat,
   ... ... and hurled myself to the ground.
   I distinctly remember looking up from that battered, prone position to see the setting sun.

CHAPTER 5: PRELUDE TO THE DESERT

The next morning I attended to my wounds and dehydration. Ahead of me lay a hot valley floor full of temporary-PCT road hiking. It was now just past dawn, and I was sweating profusely. As I stood, I saw that the road descended gradually to the valley floor.

A snake rattled his position just past one roadside boulder. Given the opportunity, my ice axe would have left him laying there.

Hours later, I was situated in a canyon of boulders that covered the trail-bed. I looked at my glasses, now in my right hand, and began to think. *Thank God the right lens did not break when I went headlong into that - that rock...* Clothed only in swimsuit, socks and boots, and dirt-clogged pores, I must have looked . . .

. . . like a PCT hiker.

Boulders eventually gave way to foliage. Although the trail was now easy to find beneath the leafy brush, the ticks in the foliage were not. Somehow the little critters had decided my legs would be a wonderful mode of transport. I didn't really notice them until I laid down to sleep that night. But I felt the stings: pain much different than those made by the prickly chaparral...

With my flashlight, I surveyed the situation. Firmly embedded in one of my upper legs was a large tick. To yank

Going Home

the critter out would mean almost certain infection, yet to 'burn him out' with the head of a hot matchstick was not too appealing, either. It took nearly ten minutes of slow-pulling in order to extricate him fully from my leg.

Days later, at Holcomb Crossing, I drank deeply at the water's edge of a horse and riders' camping area. The ticks were long since gone, but some smaller critters would now take their place, by coming along inside of me for the ride. I would not notice their giardia until almost two weeks later.

Snow patches became evident as I gained elevation. It was on one 7,000-foot elevation area in particular that I noticed a peculiar sight: cactus, as hunters' shots echoed in the distance. I dodged the many clumps of the six-inch-high prickly green stuff while hiking along an open ridgeline. *What are they doing up here?* I wondered. Stooping to look more closely and then at the map, I noticed the "reason" in the shimmering distance: the Mojave Desert was coming into view, and I would soon be thrust into it.

My feet finally brought me into the town of Acton, California, at the start of the Great Desert. My skin was a deep, dark brown. The top of my head, usually a deep, dark brown, was blonde from all the beating of the sun. I wiped the perspiration from my brow with a bandanna as I entered the town. My main thought was to find the Post Office, as I trudged along the temporary PCT just inside the city limits.

The sun was low, but the air was still very hot.

As I entered the Post Office, I was met with a blast of man-made air-conditioning. The contrast was so stark it made me cough. Putting down my pack, I retrieved my trusty wool shirt. I certainly hadn't expected to use it here!

A middle-aged lady and her small daughter had noticed my disheveled appearance. "Would you like to stay with us?" I heard her say.

My stare caused the little girl to cower next to her mom.

Going Home

"You're a Pacific Crest Trail hiker, aren't you?" she continued.

"Well yes, I am," I responded, after realizing she was talking to me.

"We marvel at the long distances you all hike. But it looks as though you haven't had a bath or a decent meal in quite a number of days."

Her demeanor was so sweet that I couldn't help but laugh. "As long as your little girl doesn't mind," I replied.

"So what does your family think about all of this?"

Conversation over the evening meal covered a variety of topics. The woman was in her early 50's, and a single mother of three children. She was also a Mormon by trade, but I would have none of her religion. Mine was out on the trail.

Six other little eyes were watching me curiously from behind their plates. "My family? Oh, they shink it'sh wonderful, more and more sho ashi make miles," I responded, in-between a bite of mashed potatoes and roast beef. "The buhlk of this schtuff," I said, swallowing, "in your living room comes from a friend up north. My Mom also keeps sending me supplements from back east. Then there's people who are excited by my progress from back south."

"But which place is your home?" Meek Mormon Mother asked.

I stopped, thoughtfully. "It used to be back east. Of more recent times it was down south. After the trail, it looks like it'll be up north."

"Well," she responded, "it's nice to have you, even if you're only passing through."

I awoke at 9 AM the next day, the longest I had slept in since the start of the trek. I was refreshed from being prone on a real mattress in this spare bedroom, after quite a long shower the night before. I got up and slowly moved over to the bedroom window to look outside. Children were playing

Going Home

in the yard. Near-by, my hostess was busy hanging laundry on a clothesline.

Going Home . . . I began to think.

I had trouble concentrating. Maybe it was the thought of the upcoming desert. Or maybe it was the bit of queasiness I felt in my stomach. Regardless, I really couldn't figure out why packing and hiking was now looking so difficult.

Until I looked at the floor.

Carpet. I looked up. Wooden dresser. I looked left. Drapes. I looked right. Painting on the wall. These things (and more) I had done without for many days now, and for many miles of traveling. I sat down at the foot of the bed, engrossed in my thoughts. It was time to move on, but for the longest time I could not move.

I was beginning to feel really sick.

"I must be off," I matter-of-factly stated to my hostess. I had just walked in-between a clothes-lined sheet and towel.

"So soon?" Meek Mormon Mother asked, somewhat surprised.

"Yes, Ma'am. I've got to make some miles today."

"Oh yes, that's right, I understand," she responded. "I forgot you have a long way to go."

CHAPTER 6:
THE DESERT
FRIDAY, MAY 08, 1981;
MILE 399.7 AT ACTON,
CALIFORNIA

In the year I hiked the PCT, there were three ways to hike from the town of Acton through the town of Mojave, which constituted the bulk of the southern-California desert stretch. The first option was to remain "true to the crest" by following the northwest, then northeast curve of the Tehachepi mountains through private land, risking injury by guards who apparently were not shy about using their guns. The second way was to follow the water piping system of the Los Angeles aqueduct, and retrieve drinkable liquid from it along the way. The third (the "PCT-alternate," and my option) was to follow the old Sierra highway along its shoulder, and stop/drink/camp in the towns of Palmdale, Lancaster and Rosamond, enroute to the town of Mojave. There would still be a long distance between water stops, but the water would definitely be there.

The first two miles out of town I felt awful. *Was it the food I ate?* And then suddenly I felt my insides tensing. "aaarrrgGGH!" I groaned. Agonizing pains shot through the pit of my stomach, doubling me over, and forcing me to lie down on the very hot pavement.

The suddenness of the pains were startling. When it seemed it hurt the most, the pains became blinding cramps, and wonder changed to groan. I started to roll. *Should I call for help?* But I could not think properly, much less call.

In-between cramps, I rolled to my knees. Up again, s-l-o-w-l-y. *WHERE AM I?* I shouted in my mind. When it rains, it ... *But it's not raining ... !*

(honk, honk) honk, Honk! Many cars had passed, but this was the first one that had -

It was my last night's family!

The driver's window rolled down. "Would you like a ride?" a familiar voice asked.

The temptation of answering 'yes' to such a question I think will be forever etched into my mind. Of course I could not accept rides, for that would mean I had "cheated" regarding hiking the entire PCT, and thus the vision would be sacked.

The problem was that I hadn't planned on getting this sick.

"We're going up to the next town," Meek Mormon Mother continued. "There's plenty of room for you and your pack in the car." As I listened, I noticed through sweaty and blinding pain, those same six small eyes I had seen across the dinner continued to peer out of the back window...

I hesitated. "N - no thank you, Ma'am. I - I need to walk this one."

"All right," she said.

And then they were gone.

The next eight miles to Palmdale were searing agony ... even worse! Every couple of minutes I would have to lay *lie* down to take a break. In-between breaks, I counted blooming desert plants, vehicles passing by, abandoned couches on the side of the road(!), rocks, ANYTHING to help keep my mind off the shooting pains.

But nothing worked.

I continued to hobble along the highway. It was the fourth day since Acton.

I collapsed into the Palmdale City Park by late afternoon that day, amidst the shouting of childrens' voices and a softball game.

More hobbling. Then Lancaster. More pavement, slow motion. Then Rosamond. More non-sights.

***

About mid-afternoon a long time later, I saw in the shimmering distance the town of Mojave. I felt like one ready-made poached egg upon reaching the city limit sign, and stopped to sit in its shade.

A few minutes later, a car pulled over on the shoulder just in front of me. "Are you one of those Pacific Crest Trail hikers?"

I looked up at him through watery salty eyes. "Yaaauum," I replied, through dry lips.

"Great." And with that, he walked back to his car, and walked back toward me, holding a bag.

"Here's a little something," he said. "One way I can help out."

Slowly, I looked inside. A plastic bottle of cold orange juice! Thankfully, I looked up.

But he was gone.

I stumbled into the Mojave City Park near twilight. It took quite a while to set up camp near the back of the park, as twilight turned rapidly to dusk. Even though there was 'artificial light' nearby in the shape of streetlamps, storefronts and restaurants, this only added to my frustration.

I went to a nearby pay phone. "Sis? Hey listen, that head umbrella you sent me for shade? I can't wear it while hiking; it hits the top of my pack! But thanks for the thought, anyway. Huh? Oh, how'm I doin'? Oh fine, a little under the weather, but fine."

Going Home

I staggered back to my camp, and collapsed onto my sleeping bag.

About 3:30 AM, it happened. I thought I was dreaming. First a noise, and then a hissing sound, and then ... ... whaaAAA?

I awoke with a start. The automatic sprinklers! I was being drenched for the first time since Mexico. *Forget the cramps! Grab the equipment, and run!*

Ten minutes later, a good fifty feet from the row of trajectiling water heads, I laid things out to dry on a nearby picnic table. *Good: nothing soaked through,* I noted. I later found out that here in desert towns they turn the sprinklers on before the sun rises, so that the water does not evaporate too quickly. (Maybe there was a sign attesting to this fact, but I never noticed it)

I laid out my sleeping bag on the ground again, and promptly collapsed back on top of it. Time passed slowly, and my mind began to drift *to the sound of rain* .. .. Mfff, huH? *WAIT A MINUTE! THIS IS NO DREAM!* I looked up and - SplooOOO**OSH!** (The *SECOND* row of sprinklers having gone off ...)

I had just received a faceful of water.

As I sat on a picnic table near the front of the park, well away from the ongoing "rain" (my gear much heavier than before), I contemplated the scene. My watch said 4:45 AM. I was drained physically and mentally. *They never wrote about this in the guidebooks,* I thought.

No, wait a minute," I stated to the air. "Maybe *I'll* write a book…"

Yeah, right.

Hot dirt roads mixed with dry trail-bed in the northern fringe of my 'desert-exit.' With each passing day, I became a little more accustomed to the searing pains rumbling inside of me. I made sure I drank lots of water and replenished my body with minerals at each rest stop. But by the time I

Going Home

reached the PCT-supply town of Weldon, California many days later, I was needing some very drastic relief.

Here ended the desert. Here began the High Sierra mountain range: the highest and most remote part of the entire PCT. By all estimates it would take nearly three weeks of hiking to reach the next PCT-supply town, and would require many extra pounds of food...

I needed to sit.

A family of four spotted me at the base of a tree just inside town. A pot-bellied man got out of the car and asked me what I was doing. But before I could say anything, a look of pity crossed Simpleton's face, and he said, "We ain't got much, but we'd shuh like'n tuh haf yu stay wid us."

I managed a weak smile.

"Weh? Whuh d'ya say?" he continued.

I couldn't say a thing. But I DID manage to maintain a smile as Simpleton loaded my pack inside the trunk.

Once inside their home, the children watched with glee as I unloaded a huge box, newly acquired from the local Post Office. I was dumping the contents right in the middle of their living room, saying, "Here, this and this and this is for you," as little arms complied. Both parents laughed.

But then a surprised look met Simpleton's face. "Won cha nee dis grub for da hike?" he asked, inquisitively. I was busy reloading my backpack as he spoke.

"This is way too much food for me," I stated. "I can't possibly carry it all."

The next morning, I was up early. Simpleton drove me to the Post Office – we arrived just as it was opening. . A large parcel scale was just outside the front door. "Why don cha step on dis scale, bodh wid and widout yer pack?" he asked me.

"Sure," I replied, moving slowly to step on the scale with my elephant-sized pack.

Once. UmmMMMph, twice. The verdict for what I would be carrying read eighty and one-half pounds exactly, or nearly two-thirds of my body weight.

"Ya be cafuh, ya heah?" he exclaimed, as I began to walk away. My knees were shaking under such a heavy load, my bowels were rumbling, and I knew I would fall over if I turned back to look.

So I waved, without looking back.

CHAPTER 7: THE CLIMB

Chunk, chunk, chunk. Up and up I trudged, along the winding switchbacks that would take me into Sequoia National Park. The weight of the pack was beginning to wear on me already ... more than the cramps, and I had only gone two miles!

Why keep going? I wondered. *Was it my willpower, or the fear of facing people if I quit? Or was it the pre-trek training, with sayings like 'Just remember Ash, each mile you hike is another $2.25 for the poison control center,' and 'Man, I tried this three times, but couldn't handle the pace, so I feel like you're doing this for me!' or even 'I'll take care of all the finances from this end...'?*

1981 was classified by the National Weather Service as a year of drought. For example, snowfall was estimated to be only 70% of what would be expected in a "normal" year. And yet reports still indicated that snowshoes might be necessary in the high country. Thus I took them, but on a couple of breaks in particular I felt like wrapping them around a nearby tree, they weighed so much.

Towering pine trees were prolific throughout the area. But never mind their shade quality, towering beauty or environmental value. The fact remained that I could not see the mountain views.

I longed for higher ground.

Going Home

On a mid-afternoon break (while again in the midst of cramping frustration), I unloaded every single item from my backpack, to see what could be eliminated. I just needed to know where all the extra weight was coming from! At times I became a raving madman, looking at my tent, my stove, my this, and my that: ALL seemed necessary!

My eyes drifted to the Psalms/Proverbs booklet stationed by my journal. I had carried it hundreds of miles, but until this time had never really looked at it. It only weighed an ounce or two, it was true, ... but – *Why did it seem so heavy?*

I gulped down an energy bar. *There,* I concluded. *THAT"LL make the pack lighter...*

The country opened up. Cramps came at infrequent intervals, so I was able to enjoy the ever-widening sights a bit. Marmots whistled as I came upon a side trail.

Like most hikers, I opted to take this side-trail up Mount Whitney, the highest mountain in the United States (outside Alaska). This was something no hiker in his right mind would want to miss; howbeit, not on the PCT itself. My plan was that once I traversed across the top of the peak, I would then descend eastward into the town of Lone Pine, California, to resupply.

At least this was the plan.

I hiked across a wide basin surrounded by the craggy heights. I was well over 10,000 feet and continuing to climb. By about dusk, I dropped camp at a frozen lake. I ate a quick dinner and got inside my bag. When twilight fell, I fell asleep to total silence, amidst billions of stars and the dark outline of jagged peaks.

The next morning I surveyed the trail, which was cut right into the base of a massive rock ridge. It was time.

As I hiked along the switchbacks that led up the wall, I would stop many times not only to admire the beauty of the panorama, but also to catch my breath. Near the crest of the narrow trail ridge atop the wall, I stopped to study a map-section of the area, noting 'thirteen thousand plus' at the elevation of "Trail Crest." Snow had just begun to fall, and I pulled out my sweater.

Now continuing up the snow-packed trail, I noticed two other hikers descending. In mid-stride, it became apparent to me that they looked nearly scared out of their wits.

"We nearly died up there!" one exclaimed.

I looked to the other.

"We hit - an ice st - storm," the other interjected, teeth chattering.

I made the summit fifteen minutes later.

On the summit, the wind and snow flurries became more intense. I moved to take cover in the large, rectangular shelter, which was packed half-full of snow. My tarp formed the carpet for my sleeping bag. Panic started to seize me, as a claustrophobic cloud came in from nowhere with a death-like intensity. I climbed into my sleeping bag without undressing. Twenty minutes later, I got out of the bag, shivering violently, heaving with cramps. *Night – mares – this – night - !* Then light began to slowly filter through a window. The glistening effect on the inside of the shelter suddenly began to glow. Panic changed to planning. "Photos!" I exclaimed. "Before the light fades!" as I ran outside.

The light didn't last more than a couple of minutes.

I went back inside, put on more clothes, jumped into my sleeping bag, and tried to close out the night. The time was 5:00 PM, June 1, 1981.

It was a long and lonely night.

I kept looking at my watch every few minutes until 5:30 the next morning, when dawn finally broke. Conditions had worsened to near white-out. To wait would have meant more panic, more claustrophobia and more darkness. My emotions could not handle that. So in order to focus on something else, I took out the map, and began to note what lay ahead.

Eight miles east, fourteen thousand feet down.

Going Home

I descended to the ice-encrusted trail leading to Trail Crest, but in actuality I had descended *below* it. *Ummmfph – head east – through the snow – can't see – (((a canyon in my way))) – ascend – finally – there's the trail...*

Wind was howling over Trail Crest when I arrived. I had to rub the inside of my glasses with a stubby-gloved finger just to be able to make out the sign. Eastward, the trail went almost straight downhill in ice-encrusted switchbacks.

As I slowly descended, my left shoulder was nearly in contact with the seemingly vertical ground: it was that steep. I used my ice-axe as a brake whenever I slipped ... which was often. Again and again I had to wipe my glasses, but it helped very little: I couldn't see much of anything.

All of a sudden, I started to lose control. Instantly, I dug the ice-axe hard into the ground to self-arrest, but it was jarred loose by a row of boulders hidden just beneath the surface of the snow.

And then I went airborne.

OH MY GOD! I screamed in my mind.

Whoomp! I made contact again with the slope on my right side. Everything moved in slow motion as I rolled onto my stomach amidst the seemingly rapid slide.

I finally pulled my head out of the snow. Back up the slope, I noticed a yellow dizziness marring my vision, along with a few stars. Slowly I stood, shaking (but not from the cold). No broken bones, bruises, or loss of pack contents, thankfully. But no 'Thank God', either. All I thought was, *Well, at least I made the journey here in record time...* So I continued eastward through knee-deep snow. I reached a canyon in short order, and turned north.

The trail was nowhere in sight.

What was it that those two had said about nearly perishing up here?

I reached another canyon, and then another. Small patches of bare ground began to break through the icy wilderness. At last, I found a small trail section sandwiched between two large snow banks, and traced the invisible extension with my eyes. Over the one bank I went, more exuberant now, as another larger trail section appeared, followed by another snow bank. The cycle was repeated again and again, until trail sections pieced together between snow banks. I could now relax my built-in directional sense.

It was well past break time, but I was too tense to stop.

I hungered for civilization.

CHAPTER 8:
LONE PINE THURSDAY, MAY 28, 1981; MILE 618.0 AT MOUNT WHITNEY, CALIFORNIA

I reached the parking lot at the trailhead by early afternoon, amidst scores of people who were waiting their turn to enter the heights. A sign on a nearby tree read "Elevation: 8,800 feet." Beyond the sign lay one lone paved road sloping down to a huge desert expanse.

"Can I catch a ride with you two?" I asked.

"Looks like you need to get dried out," one of them finally said. "Put your gear here," the other said, pointing to the open trunk.

I felt like a dried prune.

As we hit Main Street of the city of Lone Pine, the temperature read 72 degrees on a bank sign. Only 12 hours before this I was freezing.

"Here would be fine," I said.

Once I found a phone booth, I began to dial. I was sitting on the ground, barely able to make the steel phone cord reach my ear. At first I couldn't get my boots off, but with one final jerk the last one was free.

"Collect call from Ashley Pined-Out Loner. Will you accept charges?"

"Yeah! Will I? Sure! Put him on!"

"Go ahead."

Maps Man didn't even skip a beat. "Hey, Ash! Buddy! Are you where I think you are?"

"Yeah, yeah. I'm here. Just get here as soon as you can. I'll be in the city park."

By mid-afternoon the next day, Maps Man had driven the necessary mileage from San Diego. I was still drying out when he arrived.

"Hey!" he beamed. "Good to see you! How's it all holdin' out?"

"These boots are nearly shot, as you can see," I said, pointing.

"But you have another pair there," my friend retorted.

"Had 'em mailed in this box," I went on. "They're already broken in from those hikes on the beaches back in San Diego."

"Looks like you thought of everything."

Of course I hadn't, but I let it go.

"I need some money, sport. Could you spot me a twenty?"

"Sure, sure. Hey, you want to get a motel? You could rest up there better than in this park."

I considered it. "Well, I'm a bit over budget."

Maps Man cringed. "Oh, come on, Ash! Who's thinking about money at a time like this? Man, you've come quite a long way, and you look like you could use it! The dough's on me, man!"

"I – I really appreciate that," I responded. "But my support money is nearly gone."

Maps Man froze in place, not really believing me. Finally, after a long silence, he said, "So what you're saying is – "

"Is that I'm hoping she comes into some more money, so I'll have supplies further up the trail," I said, finishing the sentence for him.

Maps Man looked shocked. "SHE? You – you mean, you have a – a *woman* mailing you all your stuff?!"

I scowled and cringed at the same time. "I thought you knew," I replied. "You never met her before she moved back to Alaska, did you?"

"ALASKA?" Maps Man appeared exasperated. "Hey, who IS this, anyway?"

"An ongoing good friend," I shrugged. "And very capable of mailing things when I need them. I don't really think you could have handled the pace for mailings, anyhow."

"But what you're telling me is that you won't be able to finish this thing?" he interjected.

I let out a long sigh. "Maybe," I finally said.

A long silence ensued. Then my friend said, "Well, even if you aren't able to finish, you've still given it quite a go."

"*Dry consolation*," I muttered.

"No other out?" he asked.

"Well, there's always a loan I can get from there, and maybe even one from back east. That's probably the way I'll go." I paused, to let the impact of my words sink into my own cranium before continuing. "But it'll take years to repay it all!"

I sat in the tub until I could stand it no longer. The TV was airing some type of talk show in the background as I was drying off.

"Hey, Ash: you've gotta see this," Maps Man roared, from his comfort zone atop one of the beds.

I looked at the TV in the mirror, thinking a dozen other thoughts as I combed my hair.

The next morning I explained to Maps Man about my near brush with death atop the peak in the distance.

Maps Man started to gawk.

"And no," I interjected, "I'm not quitting. The rest last night did me good."

CHAPTER 9:
BACK UP AGAIN

"You *sure* you want to be dropped off here?"

It was early the next morning. The place was a trailhead south of Lone Pine. *Why hike a segment again?* he must be wondering. Simply put, to hike the entire trail, even if it meant overlapping sections.

I explained this to Maps Man. He looked at me with that 'you've-got-to-be-kidding' kind of look. So I added, "It's good scenery, anyway," as I removed my backpack from his trunk.

He honked, and sped off.

The trail finally gave way to a very-recognizable segment of the PCT. It wasn't long before I met the side-trail leading to Mount Whitney. No marmots whistled this time. Stopping to look up the side trail without taking off my pack, my mind went blank.

Not too far north of the side-trail to Mount Whitney, one crosses over 13,000-foot-plus Forrester Pass, the highest point along the PCT. I saw Forrester from a long way off, after fording my first torrent of a stream. At the base of the pass, I surveyed the ascent from a frozen lake, and noticed what I thought were two ways to get over the pass.

The ascent went very slowly. I would kick a step into the wall's encrusted snow three times before I could trust it enough to step up another foot of elevation. By this means,

Going Home

I would inch my way upward. Every few minutes I would pause, breathing heavily, and look downward to see what I had accomplished. It took many such pauses before I finally emerged on the height of the pass itself. Glorious!

But I had taken the wrong pass.

Now gliding down the north-face slope, I angled back toward where I thought the trail might emerge. I swished through the knee-deep snow with my fully-loaded pack firmly tightened against my back. Snow became ankle-deep as I angled to parallel the canyon that had emerged. My 'run' became a walk as exposed ground appeared. My boots and lower legs were soaked. In the distance I heard the sound of a stream, and found the trail easily.

After consuming a rather hurried dinner, I fell asleep to the sound of rushing waters.

Throughout the course of the next few days, I would slowly ascend a pass, and then descend its usually snow-laden north face. Camping would take place in the next valley area just beyond snow coverage to complete the daily 'cycle.' Average mileage per day numbered just about half of my anticipated average for the entire trek, which was to be expected in such high country. Coupled with the sometimes frequent agony of stomach cramps, I also had to contend with frozen boots at breakfast time.

Views were spectacular; each day yielded cloudless skies. I was miles from civilization, and could see why John Muir called these mountains 'the range of light.' When knee-deep snow encrusted the trail however, the walking became especially difficult. Many times I would break through the snow after painstakingly raising myself onto its delicate surface. In addition, another solo hiker complained of snow blindness.

What was that counting-the-cost thing I had heard about back in San Diego?

Going Home

On one river-crossing in particular, I decided to throw my boots across first, exclaiming, "This is the sixth crossing today! I've had enough of this!" But my second boot became a canoe when my toss landed just inches shy of the opposite side. "NO!" I yelled, racing at a full sprint down the riverbank in one bare foot. Had not an exposed rock caught it just yards shy of the river's rapid descent, I might have found this "counting-the-cost" thing impossible to fulfill. I simply shook my head during my next break. *In Boy Scouts it was a tree. Here it's a rock.*

"I just came in from a side-trail," said the father. "HE'S the one hiking this whole thing, not me."

It was late in the afternoon. Now standing before me was a two-some.

The other PCT hiker's red hair filled the pass. "Your dad come out to see you on the trail?" I asked Red.

We talked for quite a while, and then camped at one of the many alpine lakes in the area, which was teaming with trout. After two hours of fishing (the first time my fishing gear got any use), the score read: Dad five, Red two, and Ash none. *Just like in the rowboat with my own dad...* I mused.

The next day our group became one less.

"Was that a tear I saw in your dad's eye?" I asked.

"Yeah, probably," said Red. "I don't think he wanted to leave, but he had to get back home."

As the words *Going Home* filled my mind, I added, "Well, you'd probably better be getting along too. The way I'm feeling, I'd most likely slow you down."

Red paused, and then looked at me with a long stare. "What in the world are you talking about?" he finally asked.

"I'm not feeling too well," I continued. "And I know because of that I'm not going to be up to speed. So you go on ahead."

"No way, Ash – not on your life!" he forcibly replied. "I need the company. I've been without any friends on this hike for way too long."

CHAPTER 10:
BAD WATER MADE BETTER
MONDAY, JUNE 15, 1981
MILE 815.1 AT TUOLUMNE MEADOWS, CALIFORNIA

The final Sierra Nevada mountain passes went fairly smoothly for both of us, even though we still made slow time because of the snowbound north-face slopes. Red never said anything to me about my stopping to take so many bathroom breaks, but I wondered what he must be thinking. *I* was thinking, *My diet, my diet, it must be my diet...* We crossed over the last pass almost three weeks since entering the Sierra Nevadas. This was mile number "800+" for us. Numerous day hikers (in groups of 2 to 6) were heading the other way, and this was mile "0.800" for them.

"These tourists are too much," I said.

Red nodded his head.

"But the Post Office must be close!" I exclaimed.

So we quickened the pace.

At the Tuolumne Meadows Post Office, we met another "through-California" hiker while waiting in line to purchase some junk food. Random Rulesman wondered why in the world I had just bought six cinnamon rolls that had pig-fat in them.

I looked at him strangely. "There's no pork in this," I said.

"Yes there is," he replied. "See this ingredient?"

I squinted at the fine print on the label. "It says 'lard,' I finally said. "So what?"

"That's pig fat!" he exclaimed.

I wasn't too concerned at that point whether or not a pig had died or not in order to fulfill my sweet tooth. I raised my eyebrows, and just as I was about to respond to the comment, I got hit with another series of cramp attacks, and had to literally crawl to the restroom, leaving my junk food in the checkout line.

After what seemed like hours, I emerged to see Red finishing a conversation with RR, who waved at me while starting to walk away.

"So what did you think of him?" I asked Red, unbowing myself.

"Well, he kind of got grossed out by my three hot dogs. I think he didn't want to get contaminated by them."

I laughed, despite cramping pains. "So where's he going now?"

"To a health food store in the valley," Red said.

We both retrieved our resupply parcels, and sat on one of the picnic tables to open them.

"Dad!"

I looked up. Apparently, Red's family had decided that someone needed a longer vacation.

"And this must be your mom," I said. "Pleased to meet you," I continued, slowly arising from the table.

She smiled and nodded. "Would you like to ride down to the valley with us?" she asked. "We have plenty of room."

The valley: the place where most everyone in America goes if within 100 miles of Yosemite National Park (the "Half-Dome" and a towering waterfall are easily viewed from the comfort of one's car). On the one hand, I was not looking forward to having so many cars on my trail. But on the other hand, this family would be a refreshing addition to my trail.

"You know, that giardia has knocked out so many hikers," Red's dad began from behind the wheel of the car. "They've got a major article on it in the paper here." He pointed to his wife, who was reading the news. "That parasite in the water," he continued, "they say it comes from feces of animals. You really can't tell if it's in the water or not until a week or two after you drink it. Anyway, the cramps, the weakness, the loss of appetite - it's all very similar to dysentery. I can't imagine having such a thing."

My eyes went wide as Red began to ask his dad a question. *"I don't believe it!"* I exclaimed in my mind. Then I exclaimed out loud, "Stop the car!"

Luckily, a lookout point had just appeared. Once in the lot, he turned to look at Red, who in turn turned to look at me. "What's goin' on, Ash? Did you see a bear?"

"But I KNOW I've got gee-are-dee-ah, or whatever you call it! You've just got to believe me! I've got all the symptoms. And you can fix me, right?"

I was in the doctor's office. He appeared very unemotional, finally looking up at me, after scribbling something down on a pad of paper. "We have to run some tests first on your stool samples, son," he said. "But it shouldn't take long. Just wait here."

I looked out the door after him, and spotted Red in the lobby. Motioning to him with a quick jerk of my head, I quickly looked down the hall both ways.

"What is it, man? Hey, I probably shouldn't be back here."

"Yeah, I know, but listen, what your dad was talking about, I think I've got it!"

Red stopped. "You mean a bear?"

"No, man! Giardia! Now you won't have to - "

We looked up. The doctor had returned. We looked like two kids who had just been caught taking cookies from the cookie jar.

"He's my financial advisor," I finally indicated.

"Quin-a what?" I asked, looking at the pill bottle.

"Quinacrin," the doctor responded. "These pills are usually used for vaginal yeast infections, but we have found them very effective in killing the parasite that's been causing you all this pain."

I looked at the pills. Then I looked back at the doctor. Red had disappeared for a few moments. "No problem," I responded. "Just point me to a drinking fountain before my partner here gets back and starts balking about me being a female."

Red and I stayed in the main campground in the valley, while his family stayed in their camper in an adjacent campground. "Why all those bags hanging from that wire overhead?" I pointed.

"Food," Red replied. "The bears here are killers. So many people have fed them that they wait in line to land a spot for chowing down. Good old bear airport."

I could only frown.

"Take care, Ash."

I was just leaving, while Red decided to stay behind.

"We'll see you in a couple days, then?"

"In a couple days."

My first day north of Tuolumne Meadows was magnificent, due mainly to the overhaul of my insides. Hiking was indeed wonderful. Deep thoughts once blocked by cramps now surfaced. I stopped at a waterfall whose sparkling water crossed the trail. I dipped my sierra cup into the stream.

I stared down into the confines of the clear liquid now in my cup. I had plenty of pills in my backpack, just in case the water was infected. I took a deep drink, and then another. But something was missing, and my insides knew it. I began to sense for the first time that this hike would not end at Canada.

Standing up, I heard only silence. It was time to leave.

The last thing I remembered thinking was that I needed something else to drink.

CHAPTER 11:
HIGH AND DRY
FRIDAY, JULY 10, 1981
MILE 1,175.5 AT THE FEATHER RIVER:
HALFWAY (MILEAGE) POINT OF THE PCT

Northern California was drier than the Sierras. There were many dusty logging roads in-between the trail sections. Shade was scarce.

The guidebooks were faithful up to a point regarding the pinpointing of water sources. I say up to a point because 1981 was classified as a year of drought. Supposed springs were bone dry as I meandered my way through the country. One dribbling spring in particular required pushing my sierra cup into the ground at an angle, in order to catch small drops of water.

It was a long, hot and uncomfortable section.

At one ridgeline area in particular, I surveyed the map for just exactly where a water spring was supposed to be. 'Down the ridge just a tad, and off to the right...' But I never did find the dribbling life source, which was supposed to flow all year (said so right there in the guidebook).

A large pumice rock protrusion surrounding the site began to laugh at me. I had but one pint of water left, and the next source of water would entail many more hours of hiking in the sweltering summertime heat.

I sat down on a tree stump, and stared at my backpack. My eyes traveled to a small, smooth pebble at the base of the stump. I immediately grabbed it as a man would a treasure, and washed it. Then into my mouth it went, to activate saliva.

Going Home

Upon rising, the back part of my legs stuck to the stump. The cost factor this time? Tree sap. All the more accentuated by the stifling heat.

Dust rose to meet my knees at every movement. I was later to learn that trees had been cut down for economic reasons, which made the PCT section that I was on nothing more than a logging road.

Removing the pebble from my mouth, I proceeded to consume half my remaining water supply. That left me with only a cupful. And the map showed five miles, or over two hours of hiking to go, for more water.

Hopefully.

Thirty more minutes passed. I thought I heard the distant sound of rushing water. The map indicated that the PCT would soon descend in long, slow switchbacks to the Feather River. A rush of adrenaline surged through me, as I correlated the distant noise with the river on the map.

In another twenty minutes I reached the start of the switchbacks. Cotton was forming in my mouth, so I consumed the rest of my water in one fell swoop. Then after ANOTHER 30 minutes of hiking the long arcs, I stopped to rest. My heart was beating wildly, as my whole body screamed for thirst.

This was the beginning of the deepest pain I had ever known. There was no way to cut the switchbacks. "WHERE ARE YOU?!" I screamed to the river, far below me. My daily routine of 50 minutes hiking and 10 minutes resting went out the state of California as I started to run the trail, which kept arcing in nearly parallel swaths in-between switchbacks. The dull roar of the Feather River ever-so-gradually increased in volume.

I sat down again. "God, help!" I yelled. "I can't cut this!!"

I opened my pack, and then all plastic water bottles in an attempt to glean a few more drops of precious liquid.

Of course, there were none.

Going Home

I hastily shoved items back into the pack. Now arising, slamming the pack against my back, I ran in nearly a full trot along the trail. After a few more minutes, the footpath finally leveled out.

But the river was nowhere in sight.

My mind started to drift to a race of long ago: a 26-plus mile marathon that had left me dehydrated, hallucinating one mile from the finish line. I had finished, but barely so. It had taken nearly six hours of vomiting and replenishing of liquids for my system to return to normal.

I shook myself. Off the side of the trail – faded at first, but then slowly coming into focus – I noticed – wet – greenery! Instantly swooping down to it, while throwing my pack off at the same time, I pressed my face into the moss, hoping to extract some precious moisture.

But this procedure only succeeded in making my cracked lips green.

"aaaAAAHHH!" I screamed.

I grabbed my backpack by the straps and dragged it up the trail. After only a few seconds I fell to the ground, panting heavily.

I knew I was dying. All that talk in high school about our bodies being made up of more than 90% (70%) water finally began to make sense. I shook my head and listened intently. The river sounded – close. Over to the side of the trail, it looked – well, wet. I had to squint in order to begin to focus. But as my eyes did focus, I saw something.

What was that ... ?

I shook my head again. There. There! A small dribble of water coming off the side of the trail ...

BREAK TIME!!!

My sierra cup got very good use. I placed it underneath the dribble, and time and time again it went to my lips. Minutes passed, but I don't know how many. Then finally turning onto my knees with my pack, I pushed with extra

Going Home

effort to stand up. Now on wobbly knees and shaky stature, I began my journey again: toward Canada, on the PCT.

200 feet and one minute later, I came to the Feather River itself.

Flashback. Southern California: a few weeks prior. One stop at a stream of river and sand, where I literally spent over an hour filtering and refiltering the mixture through a bandanna to drink, only to find 200 feet ahead and one minute later was a clear and sparkling river.

I stopped just below the bridge to take off my boots and socks so I could immerse my feet in the running waters. Rinsing and ringing-out my sweat-clogged socks (one inner-liner pair and one wool pair) was my 'washing machine' out on the trail. It took me longer than usual to tie all four socks to the top of my backpack so they could dry in the sun. Pulling out the trailguide from the top zipper pouch to see what would be next, I noticed some interesting numbers.

5,900 feet of elevation gain in less than 10 trail miles, with zero gallons of water along its length.

I closed my eyes, and waited for God only knows how long.

I then noticed the sky.

All was still.

As I ascended, my eyes focused on the ground immediately in front of my feet. From time to time I would glance up the trail in order to see the next 'ascent-section' before staring again at the trail just in front of my feet. I counted paces as I walked. The bugs, the heat, the weight of the pack, the memories of cramps and recent dehydration, the sweat and all the aches were somehow put into perspective as I began to hum an inspirational song from pre-trek days. I was back on my 50/10 schedule, and after four couplets, the end of the ascent was in sight.

Once arriving, I slowly removed my pack to sit on the overlook named "Lookout Rock." I drank in the surrounding landscape, which extended hundreds of feet down and also outward many miles, to the horizon. Trees dotted the landscape, but even at this distance they still looked dusty and dried out. Waves of tiredness began to sweep over me as the prior 'twenty-torrid miles' began to sink into my brain. Such a place would be ideal to lay down my sleeping bag and call it a day, except for one thing.

Water was nowhere in sight.

On and on I trekked. Cattle dotted the next forest I encountered, and we stopped what each of us was doing in order to survey the other. After about three long seconds, I heard this massive clanging of cowbells as the herd scattered.

By the time I reached for my camera they were gone.

I decided upon a late lunch at a babbling brook (with no space to camp). Stoking up my small white-gas stove, I boiled water to make some instant soup. (What can I say? I like hot soup, even in the sun.)

After lunch, I began to hike again, this time on a level pathway. Twilight was closing in. I hiked another few miles before finding a reasonable campsite near a flowing stream surrounded by trees. Spreading out my ground cloth and sleeping bag on top of it, I laid on the bag itself. I breathed a long sigh of relief that this twenty-three-plus mile day was now over, and proceeded to rub my weary legs.

I then contemplated what it would be like to finish. But in the middle of the contemplation my mind went blank.

CHAPTER 12:
IS THIS REALITY, OR WHAT?

In the confines of Lassen Volcanic National Park in extreme northern California, the PCT meandered through a number of road crossings. They had no names.

So where's the real trail? I wondered, in passing.

The going had been very hot. Shade was minimally evident in burnt-out pine trees. I was beginning to wonder who gave the status of "national park" to such an area.

So where's the real wilderness? I wondered, in passing.

Not long after entering the park, I rounded a bend in the main footpath, and stopped. Here was a lake that was bright pea-green in color. Furthermore, it was over 130 degrees (according to the guide-book), and very undrinkable.

So where's the real water? I wondered, in passing.

Mount McGlaughlin came into view in another short while up the trail. Bugs were prolific, and began to feast on me in the dripping heat. The PCT was now composed of very lightweight and crusty pumice, deep-red in color: great for the looks, but murder for the ankles.

So where's the REAL trail? I yelled to my mind, in passing.

Suddenly a thought shot through my mind like an unexpected bullet. This trail I had been hiking on for months was more than a 24-inch wide footpath: it had come to symbolize everything from the views to the lack of views, from the proliferation of water to the areas of drought, from the giardia to the fixes, from the weight of the backpack to the parcels at Post Offices, from the vision of the actual hiking to the conditioning leading up to it and to the dreams that lay beyond. It was something I had never fully considered, even while spending all those prior years in college.

Even though it was monotonous, walking along the highway revealed close-ups of things you simply could not see, for example, screaming along it in an automobile. The guidebook presented this option at the Hat Creek Rim route, since polluted water and no shade were along its route. Raspberry bushes and lost pennies were some of the 'treasures' I found along this road-segment of the PCT. A tattered, abandoned couch even formed the basis for one of my breaks.

The segment ended at Burney Falls State Park. My feet were quite sore from all of the pavement pounding. And the sign at the entrance booth said you could rent a plot of land for ten dollars that would house much more than I was carrying.

But there was nothing cheaper.

I told the clerk at the booth that I wanted to see the campground first. She shrugged and said fine. So I walked through the park, amazed by the sight of so many people and so much excess baggage.

At an unsuspecting campsite, I asked, "Could I buy that corner of your plot for a couple of dollars?"

The couple sitting outside their RV looked up. Then the man smiled. "And I suppose you want to buy some of this here white gas for the same amount, instead of an entire gallon?" he asked, waving the can.

I laughed. *Here's someone who understands...*

"I'll tell you what," he continued. "You set your things over there, come fill up your stove and fuel bottle, and have some grub with us. In payment, we want to hear all about your hike."

I leaned my pack against a nearby tree, and then sat down at the picnic table. I gratefully consumed the treat. When I finally bit into the mass for the second time and looked up, the couple was staring at me.

"Guess you're probably wondering what I'm doing all the way out here," I commented.

He smiled, and said, "Not if you're trying that PCT I've read about!"

Good, I thought, *Minimal introductions...*

"Yes, that's right," I replied.

The man leaned forward from his lawn chair, and asked, "So what about when you finish?"

I paused, in the middle of a bite. "What do you mean?"

He locked eyes with me. "What are you going to do when this is all over?"

My tired eyes were unable to focus. "Well, I tried to think about that earlier. But it's like air in my hand – it leaves the moment you try to grab it."

The man looked at his wife. "I think you'd better sleep on it," he said.

But it was too noisy in the tourist-infested park to sleep well that night.

CHAPTER 13: HUT IN THE STAR-STUDDED HILLS

The town of Sawyers Bar, in extreme northern California, boasted the smallest Post Office I encountered along the trail. It actually looked more like a shack. My boots had just touched upon a road crossing – the closest point of approach to the town itself – when I realized the distance to the shack. To hitchhike this road a few miles into town would not be "cheating" though, since a side-trip is not part of the PCT itself.

In short order, a small (and very well-used) pickup appeared, stopping just ahead of my thumb. Two men motioned for me to climb into the back of the truck. I had just sat down when I was jerked into reality by a sudden takeoff, and then pinned into wide-eyed splendor as the little beater raced through the curves of the road at a harrowing speed. When we reached the town of Sawyers Bar, I jumped out of the pickup, eyes still wide. "You - you ALWAYS drive like that?!" I asked, in amazement.

"The only excitement we ever get," the Nameless Nomads remarked.

My parcel was intact at the post office, even though I was told I might have to wait until the next day to retrieve it. "Unless you hurry, sonny," said the clerk, "'Cuz we close in five minutes." The clock read 12:55 PM. *Is this legal?* I

Going Home

wondered, noting their 10 AM opening time. Well, no matter: dismiss the thought and get your box!

Thirty minutes later, everything from it was stuffed into my pack, and all the extras were boxed to mail back north. But I would have to wait another day for the postmaster.

In the General Store, while looking for items not available either in supply-parcels or out on the trail, I heard a voice behind me. "You're a Pacifih Cress Traal hikah, arn cha?"

I turned to see a man much taller and younger than I.

"Yep," I replied.

"Guhd. Wanna stay wit me fer th' naat? Ah've gotta place in me cabin up yonda," he drawled, pointing over his shoulder through the storefront window, to the hills beyond.

"Well, ... sure," I said, but then added, "as long as you can drop me off back on the trailhead tomorrow morning, and then take this here box to the PO to mail. By the way, how fast do you drive?"

The man scratched his head. "Say whah?"

It took quite a while to get within sight of his cabin. "It gets kinda lonely up heah," he said, "but ah do Uh Kay."

A series of bumps in the old dirt road nearly crunched my head on the roof of his truck. When I finally settled back down, we hit another bump. When I came down and grabbed the dash, he laughed a drawl. "Graht rads, thes!" he yelled.

But I wasn't so sure.

A domicile finally appeared: the only place for miles. Shutting off the truck, he said, "C'mon in." He was already heading for the front door, or back door, or whatever it was.

A fire was brewing as I walked in the cabin door with my pack. Collapsing on the couch, waves of tiredness instantly began to sweep over me. I sat, staring at the walls of the first home I had been in for God-only-knows how long.

My host finally finished the fire, and then sat down across the room from me. He smiled as warmth began to fill the

Going Home

cabin. I pointed, and asked, "You play that, or is it just for looks?" Without hesitating, he reached over and picked up a guitar, and began strumming a ballad about a night filled with stars. I leaned back, arms behind my head, and grinned a huge smile.

"Now remembuh," he said. "Y'all keep hikin' and donna quit. And remembuh me when ya finish, hokay?"

It was early the next day. The man with the hut in the star-studded hills had just driven me to the PCT-trailhead. "Well, I can't promise you that your name'll be in print, but I will make reference to you," I said.

In the days that followed, I rarely saw another soul. Although I was quite able to follow the guidebook maps and trail descriptions through all the northern California territory, I was not quite able to "see" the PCT through all of the temporary road sections. Even so, the flavor I found in hiking through northern California reminded me of being transported back in time. The woods even had a rustic flavor all their own. I envisioned cabins hidden back among the trees. When I would pass a logging road where there were people, they all looked, well, country.

A bird whistled. I stopped to view the sight. And for one brief moment, I realized why I had paid such a price to hike the entire PCT. But then the moment was gone, and I retreated back into step-patterns long engrained into my psyche from the Mexican border.

Near Sonora Pass (a PCT road crossing), I ascended from a long viewing distance while a few tourists stood outside their vehicles where the pass met the road. When I finally arrived at the pass itself, I explained to them just what I was doing. Staring in disbelief, and then clapping and whooping, they let me know that they wanted to be a part of the hike too.

"Hoo-boy," minced one heavy-set man, in-between bites of a hot dog. "I wouldn't want YER shoes for nothin'!" He took another bite.

"Rollo!" yelled a lady. "Swallow your food!"

This brought more clapping and whooping from the nearby tailgate party. The accolade was nice, but I had to admit that the lemonade they offered me was even better.

I finally bid them adieu, and took off hiking north on the PCT to a ridgeline. In only a few minutes (after gaining sufficient elevation), I stopped to review the pass and the party of six. But they had left. I took out my logbook to write.

Glancing at my calendar, I noticed that the summer was more than half gone.

First Boy Scout Camping Trip, c. 1970.

Author in Anza, California, on first PCT layover, one week into the trek.

CHAPTER 14:
IGLOOS, OR HIKING?
THURSDAY, JULY 30, 1981
MILE 1,534.1 AT SEIAD
VALLEY, CALIFORNIA

The last PCT resupply point before exiting California was in a small town called Seiad Valley. This cozy little place laid smack against three sets of peaks named after devils. Once hikers left the town, they would ascend over 5,000 feet in a relatively short distance to round them.

I spotted a pay phone just down the street from the Post Office, shortly after my arrival in town. I grabbed for the phone, and punched in the numbers.

"Collect call from Ashley Pacemaker. Will you accept charges?"

"Hey, WOW, yeah, I will!" exclaimed a San Diego voice.

"Go ahead."

"Ash! Is that really you?!"

Without hesitating, I said, "Yep, it's me! But I'm tired, sport."

"Wha - " Then there was this long pause. "Are you - are you quitting?" he finally asked.

"No, not that," I responded, fading off into silence.

"Well, you don't sound like it," he snorted.

"Well, I'm not, in some ways. I don't even know if I could make a book flow, based on what I'm feeling now."

"Hmmm. Well, all right, Ash. But why in the world are you worried about writing a book?"

Going Home

Silence.

"I can make some calls for you if you want me to."

I sighed. "Yeah, make some calls."

Enroute back to the Post Office, my mind began to drift to statistics encompassing my last sigh. Less than 35 through-hikers would sign the trail register in this town. The other 175 or so dropped out either from physical sickness, physical weariness, home sickness, emotional overload, or lack of funds. They were all ...

Going home...

"You going to stand there all day, sonny, or do I have to climb over you?"

I turned my head. My thoughts were so engaged that I forgot I was blocking the door to the Post Office. I was in a nice old lady's way.

"Uh, yeah."

I gave her my place in line.

The trail register had my attention from the word go. I saw a couple familiar names, and then one unmistakably familiar. *I don't believe this...* I mused. *He got here THAT fast?* This particular through-hiker I met on the PCT road-section near the Hat Creek Rim cutoff. I recalled our first meeting, near that Rim ...

"So, YOU'RE Ashley!"

I had just stopped at a General Store along the road. The voice startled me, and I whirled around, saying, "Huh?!"

"I've been chasing you the last three Post Offices!" he continued.

I hadn't noticed. "Chasing me?" I asked.

"You've been a tough one to catch," No-Time continued, reaching for a soda. "I started much later than you, and I've been charting your progress at each trail register. It's been a good challenge!"

"So - so we're in a race?" I asked.

"Well, of course, with the weather and all," he replied. "But having someone pace me makes it that much more interesting!"

He was one week ahead of me, the Seiad Valley trail register indicated. I had wanted to stay with No-Time for awhile, but I really didn't want to maintain his 30-mile-per-day average. I caught him at mile number 27 the day after we met, but he kept going past 30, and I never saw him again after that.

Probably just as well, I thought. *Might miss out on a few things.*

Like well feet.

I retrieved my parcel, went back outside, cut open the wrapping tape that surrounded the box, and pawed through the box like a child with a new toy. After a few of the Styrofoam packing peanuts began to race down the street, I went back inside the building. I pulled out item after item, and stacked them by my backpack while in turn throwing away all the rest of the packing. As I reached the bottom of the box, I found a letter, which read: "All the effort of packing boxes is worth it," Pro Verbs indicated, "since you are coming to Alaska to live, once the journey is through."

Was I? I couldn't remember how I had decided that. I only recalled mentioning that I had nowhere else to call home after the hike during a phone call to her when I was back in central California. I looked at the letter again, and re-read it. *Why was this letter making me mad? Is it because I have no home? And what about all the igloo-type domiciles in the far north? Could I really handle such an after-trail life?!*

The more I pondered the situation, the more my first days with Pro Verbs came to mind. This woman had tricked me into giving her a ride home form a work-related function the first night we met, by conveniently forgetting to bring her car. We had stopped by the La Jolla (northern San Diego) beach to take a walk, and she had reached over to kiss me.

Like a dumb ox, I had agreed to stay with her that night,... and many more to follow.

"Proverbs Chapter Seven."

I stopped. *Who - what was that?*

I looked up to see the usual business that was taking place in the Seiad Valley Post Office lobby. It appeared to me that no one else had heard anything. I could have sworn, though, that *I* had heard something.

Reaching inside the pack, I located the little bible in the top zipper pocket – that little 'security' item I carried, but had never looked at. In the table of contents, I found Proverbs. Then I found Chapter Seven.

I read about halfway through the storyline before nearly slamming the little book shut.

The next day, I staked out a place in the Laundromat, clothed only in a swimsuit and SCUBA-booties. Everything else was making the rounds in a nearby washing machine. I passed the time by writing postcards. Then I headed back to the city's only park, to complete the day's layover.

Two other hikers were there when I arrived. One was from the Midwest, and the other hailed from Colorado. They motioned for me to come over to their camping spot. The one from Colorado spoke first.

"We did most of it," he stated, referring to hiking the entire PCT, "but the desert we skipped. I mean, it looked really boring!"

"Well it was, along the roads," I commented, taking out a fishnet-style stuff sack.

The other hiker was intrigued. Mellow Mover had not moved since I had come on the scene, but now he leaned forward to get a closer look at what I was holding. Apparently he had never seen a see-through stuff sack before.

"Hey, man," he drawled. "What's that for, the ven-tih-LAY-shun?"

I stopped to look at him, his sunglasses and his beaming smile. "It's a free gift from my employers," I responded, ignoring the tone of the question. "They didn't have a gold watch at the time."

We talked a while longer. 'Avoid Deserts' was born and raised in Boulder, Colorado, which lay just east of the Rocky Mountains. He had seen his share of scenic wildernesses, and spoke like he might skip some more territory up north. Mellow Mover, on the other hand, had never seen a mountain before, having been born and raised in Lincoln, Nebraska. He had tagged up with his former college buddy at the last minute, thinking such a hike would be "cool." "But in the desert it got hot," he was quick to say, "and so, like wow, we skipped it."

"Time to eat and sack out," I finally stated. "Nice talking with you two."

"Yeah!" Mellow Mover chirped back. "Maybe we can hike together! I mean, that'd be really cool!"

"I get up early," I matter-of-factly stated. *How in the world did they make it this far?*

Before the sun creased the trees the next morning, I was off. The first section of 'trail' was Main Street through Seiad Valley. RV's dotted the road. A few people and their dogs were outside of their chariots. *It's too early for this,* I thought. But then I stopped. An old lady in a lawn chair on the sidewalk smiled at me as I came near the last Main Street camper. "Oh, little Ralphie wouldn't hurt anybody!" the old lady chirped.

"Then – then why's your dog growling at me like that?" I asked, ice-axe ready.

"Oh sonny, his hair just naturally stands up this time of the day."

Yeah, right. "Well, then, you won't mind just holding your dog while I pass by?"

Going Home

She laughed. I didn't. "He doesn't bite," she insisted, not even moving to hold her pet.

The dog, a small little poodle-type terrier, moved toward me, teeth barred. I stopped. He growled. I "chiNKED!" my ice-axe into defense position. Emotions similar to the Mount Whitney whiteout came into view, as I continued to stare at the two little angry eyes in front of me.

My ice axe was certainly becoming a very handy tool in more ways that one.

"Now *now* ralphy, RALphy boy, stay here, boy," she calmly uttered. The dog stood still, and followed me with his head as I slowly walked by. I turned to walk backwards after passing him. *Crazy dog,* I fumed. *Why, a bear might be more welcome out here...*

After gaining sufficient distance from the RV, I turned to see if good old Ralphie was trying to tag along. (He wasn't) I kept looking back as I hiked, until I had left the town perimeter.

It suddenly occurred to me that my disheveled appearance, from so long on the trail, was what probably set the dog off.

Onward.

CHAPTER 15:
THE OREGON DESERT
MONDAY, AUGUST 10, 1981
MILE 1,709.3 AT CRATER
LAKE, OREGON

Now safely out of town, the PCT trailhead was next. "Lookout devils, here I come!"

After only a short while, the ascending trail began to level out. I looked out over the valley from a viewpoint during the ascent. All other views were blocked by trees.

I kept hiking, through a forest.

Another road crossing. A gold miner's camp. A pond of a lake, undrinkable. These were passed in rapid succession. A red and white sloping "peak" named Kangaroo Mountain was encountered next near a dirt road crossing. By mid-afternoon during one of my ten-minute breaks, I noted in the trailguide that I had traveled over 23 miles that day. I rubbed my eyes and counted again. *Yep, twenty three plus,* I mused. And there still was quite a bit of sun left in the sky. Why wasn't I tired? What was happening? Was this the calm before the storm?

My campsite that night was in an abandoned park, cut through by old logging roads. The park looked at one time like it had been well-populated with kids on swings, parents roasting hot dogs on grills, dogs barking.

But here it sat: dormant, quiet, rusting ...

The next day, I sang a few songs to keep in rhythm with my step. I tried to make sense of the Pacific Crest Trail here, which definitely was not on the crest of any mountains. One step, two step, that's all I gotta do, step...

A few days later, through some clear-cut areas and a ranch-like farm, I uneventfully entered the state of Oregon. I had hiked 60% of the entire PCT: nearly 1,600 miles, and here I was, in the non-signed end of an empty horse pasture with a few flowers. *The map says the border's just - about – here.* "Ye-haw!" I yelled to the sky, fist upright.

It was a lonely celebration.

More forest. More non-forest through a clear-cut (now treeless) section. The last views of Mount Shasta in extreme northern California. And then another thicker forest which went on for a long time. I remember wondering again when the whole viewless adventure would end. Minutes became hours. Paces were counted, but my boots ended up tripping on tree roots with greater and greater frequency. The map was little help what with all the tree cover. Finally though, I came to a major highway crossing, complete with signs indicating 'civilization' nearby, in the form of a town.

The name of the town was Ashland, some five or ten miles north. It hosted a Shakespearean festival at the time of my highway crossing. Tourists would be numerous there. I opted for the nearby restaurant indicated in the guidebook, in order to think things over.

As I walked into the restaurant, I was overcome with amazement at a table-full of PCT hikers, busy feasting on an overflowing banquet. *Where did they all come from?* I wondered, as two of them motioned for me to pull up a chair. As I sat down and ordered my meal, I discovered through the course of ensuing conversations that every person seated at the table claimed to be Mexico-to-Canada hikers.

"Round six, Ash!" exclaimed one.

"Hard work: this!" ranted another, as his fork was raised for the umpteenth time.

Going Home

I stared for only a short time at the ongoing circus before launching into my dinner.

A few days after the road crossing, I came alongside a mountainous volcanic protrusion named Pilot Rock. It was there I met up with a man and a woman hiking the entire PCT together, and shortly afterward discovered they were both hiking it for the second time around.

I was dumbfounded. "Why are you doing it again?" I finally asked.

"Because," Second-Time-Around matter-of-factly stated. "And besides, my girlfriend and I relate better out here. And then there's Thielsen Creek, which is quite deluxe."

"Huh?" I said, surprised.

"You'll see what I mean later," he added.

We made our way through the sparse forests of southern Oregon, complete with desert sand, in good time. Or was it crushed pumice? The merciless heat combined with the scarcity of water to cause me to long for the heights. Springs, scarce as they were, dribbled in so-called ponds, requiring extra purification before consumption. Giardia thankfully didn't find me, but the clear-cuts did.

Clear-cuts. Again and again, we noted landscapes that had been scarred from the elimination of all trees by economically-minded logging companies. In the place of such towering wonders they left stumps. The trail made haphazard weavings just to traverse the landscape, in-between and amongst the exposed root systems of the trees. 'It's still part of the PCT,' we had to remind ourselves.

We all knew that. And so we hiked it.

We finally entered the confines of Crater Lake National Park amidst record high temperatures in the lower 90s. The Second-Time-Around couple had been a welcome addition to my Oregon trail. They refused to get down because of some uneventful sections of the PCT.

"Where's the lake?" I asked.

"Oh, it's up that hill," she responded.

"But the PCT says we go *this* way!" I retorted.

"You don't want that. You'll miss all of Crater Lake if you take it."

"Wha - ?" I was stunned.

"The reason they do that," he said, "is because the rim road around the lake doesn't qualify for PCT standards of solitude and scenic wilderness. And the lay of the land is such that you would not see the lake if you adhered to the footpath. Hence, this designated alternate, which we are now taking the second time around. Didn't you read about it in the guidebook?"

I obviously hadn't, or hadn't paid too much attention to it. I grunted, and then asked, "So what do we do now?"

"We get deluxe!" exclaimed Second Time Around, as he took to scale the hill.

Crater Lake did not come into view until we were right upon the rim, as my companions had indicated. The slope of the hill leading up to the view, coupled with the dramatic drop-off from the rim-road to the lake itself, made for an instant panorama, pummeling all the senses at once.

"This is really something," I said.

"That it is," they chimed.

But then I asked, "So how do you get water from it to drink?"

They laughed. "The water faucet at the main lodge, Ash."

So much for reality...

"You mean to tell me that the next water is HOW far away?!"

"Twenty five miles," Second-Time-Around quipped. "But once you reach Thielsen Creek, it's deluxe. You wait and see."

"Through more desert?"

"It's worth it though, Ash," replied his girlfriend, ignoring my comment. "Just keep putting one foot in front of the other, just like before, and you'll get there. Just one long day, that's all."

"Just one long day...?" My head sank. *So where am I going to find water bottles to carry extra water?* I looked around me, wondering. All that was evident were campers, tourists, more campers, more tourists, and trash cans. *Trash cans.* I went over to the nearest one, and spotted two one-gallon plastic milk jugs, empty.

They would work.

We found campsites in a park by the lodge. Inside the lodge, a dance was happening. But somehow, it seemed out of place, and I sacked out early.

That night I had a dream about eating sand.

CHAPTER 16:
THE LIGHTNING ROD OF THE CASCADES

"**W**e're going to layover here *another* day?" I asked, concerning the lodge.

"No, we'll just wing it," replied Second-Time-Around, as he looked toward the lodge. "Which reminds me: there's someone you need to meet."

This other through-hiker I had read about prior trail registers. He was shorter and skinnier than I (at 5'9" and 140 lb.) and had a backpack that towered over my own elephant-sized pack. All we could see in approaching him from the backside was a massive canvas bag atop two matchstick legs housed in running shoes.

He turned. On his head was a wing-footed cap.

"I was going to quit after California," he said, "but here I am!"

He caught me staring at his cap.

"Listen, I don't run, but I would like to finish."

The Second-Time-Around couple, Wing Foot, and I had a good time that afternoon exchanging stories over cokes in the lodge cafeteria. I could imagine myself finishing the trail with these three.

"Look," I finally said. "Why don't we all hike up the road a piece to see if we can't get closer to 'The Watchman' lookout? I'd like to see the lake in the morning sun, if that's OK with you all."

A three-fold pause. "But there's no place to camp there," said Wing Foot, in-between the belch of a coke and a frown. "So count me out."

"You two, too?" I asked.

"Afraid so, Ash."

Another pause. "Well," I continued, "I'll take a photo for you."

The sunrise the next morning was glorious. I had found a suitable place to camp well off the road, despite Wing Foot's statement. At the first hint of light, I had scurried out of my sleeping bag, hurried up the short trail that ascended to the lookout tower, and had arrived just as the sun creased the horizon. I was fascinated to find a ranger wide-awake inside the tower, busy with paperwork.

Time stood still as I sat on the concrete barrier overlooking Crater Lake. Even a wide-angle camera lens would not be able to fit the entire lake on a print. Soon, a few birds appeared, and soared in front of and away from me.

Straps all cinched in place, I began my early morning hike in silence. Road in time gave way to trail, as the Oregon Desert began to fill the landscape. I wasn't supposed to take any pumice with me through Crater Lake National Park, but a lot of it stuck to my legs. Pine trees gradually began to fill the landscape, overtaking the desert, and the resultant shade helped to provide at least some relief from the merciless heat. I began to wish I had waited for the other three hikers.

Eventually coming to a side trail, I noted a sign: "Water – one-half mile." I stopped, and removed my pack. My back was soaked with sweat.

One half mile? I thought to myself. And what happens if it's dry? That's a good half hour wasted!

I stood there only a moment before strapping myself back in. The sweat-soaked exterior of the pack was amazingly cold. My mind was gawking at the contrast.

The dry country is a funny place. If you have your sights set on comfort in any form while walking outside, those sights will soon be brought into focus. I never saw a house or a camper or anyone throughout the entire area, and this only accentuated the dryness.

Late in the day (pine trees having grown to a more respectable height), I encountered another side trail. This one did not lead to a spring. Rather, it led upward. "Thielsen Peak: One Mile" was firmly etched into a sign at the junction. It only took a moment to decide on another view despite the lack of water. Since Thielsen Creek was not too much farther up the main trail and I still had sufficient water, I decided to give it a go. I just hoped that the 'deluxeness' of Thielsen Creek would splash its way into my life after the climb. I didn't need another Feather River experience.

Stashing my backpack, I started up the side-trail with only a fanny pack enclosing compass, trail mix and water. The trail soon became steep, and finally emerged upon an open valley of volcanic rockslides.

I met someone coming down off the mountain on a scree slope. Diamond Lake was shimmering in the distance behind me as we met.

"Here, read this," he said, handing me a small guidebook. *'This portion,'* it began, *'is what separates the men from the boys. Once you find the large crack on the backside, shinny your way up through it to the peak itself,'* was essentially what it said.

I finished reading the entire account. Then looking up, I asked him, "Did you go?"

"No way!" he exclaimed. "I'm not THAT crazy. I suggest you forget it!"

I went anyway.

Standing on top, I shouted a shout of victory to the waters of Thielsen Creek far below. But then I immediately dropped down on all fours, sensing the loss of balance. The peak was the size of a small tabletop, and dropped off steeply on three of its four sides! Quickly scurrying back down through the eighty-foot crack, it was time to get to camp.

While descending, I noticed something out of the corner of my eye. It was on a nearby ridgeline that ran south from Thielsen, and seemed - well, very much out of place. As I moved closer to get a better look at it, something from one of my Sunday school days came into view.

Someone had constructed a cross on top of the ridge.

Wha -?

As I continued to descend the scree slope, one thought, in the form of a question, filled my mind.

Did someone die up here?

CHAPTER 17:
AN HONEST HIKE

It was just after twilight as I stumbled upon Thielsen Creek. I was astounded to find about 20 other hikers camping there. Over half of them immediately surrounded me. They wanted to know what the peak had been like, which was now in the distance as a golden-hue.

"The Lightning Rod of the Cascades, I hear!" one said.

"Yeah, good thing it wasn't raining!" another chimed.

"So how hard *was* it?" asked a third.

"Hey, give him some space, will you?" another voice replied.

I turned. This 'voice' and his Second Time Around girlfriend had saved a campsite for me, away from 18 others.

"Thanks," I said. "But is this what you meant by deluxe?"

"Sort of," he stated. "But further up the trail, it gets better."

"Where's Wing Foot?" I asked.

"Still at the lodge. His parents came down to visit."

I paused. "Why so many – other people?"

"They came in droves, Ash, about an hour before you got here," he replied. "Apparently, most hiked in from Diamond Lake."

"Any through-hikers?"

"A few," he said. "But by the way they talk, I'm not sure if they're telling the truth."

With no way to tell. I thought. And then I thought, *Well, just how DOES one 'prove' it?* Even by keeping meticulous journals, describing every ridgeline, tree and blade of grass would not do it, since you could fudge that from existing literature, and market it accordingly. And a thousand witnesses could be at your side at the Canadian border, testifying to your having 'done it', but unless they hiked every step with you (and took continuous videos besides), only God would know in the final tally if you were being honest. Hikers like Eric Ryback, for example (who claimed to be the very first person to hike the distance, amidst much controversy) would have to deal with that.

"Yeah: it burns me up," I finally said.

But then again, I thought, *what's the big deal here?* In other words, why is it so important to "prove" to others that this was an "honest" hike? Oh sure, there's the walk-a-thon mileage tallies, and the journals for companies who gave equipment, - but – we're all so – so DRIVEN out here! *Was this some sort of competitive pride? Or was it for some sort of a 'status-symbol,' minus a 21-gun salute?*

"What was that you said?" Second-Time-Around asked.

I shrugged my shoulders. "This is too much," was all that I could say.

"Come again, Ash?"

"I'm trying to, Second Time," I responded. "I'm really trying."

Dawn was approaching. I slowly rustled myself out of my sleeping bag and stood up. Then silently rolling up my sleeping bag, I positioned the pack on my back and took off north again, munching on a meatless pemmican bar. No one else in the entire camp had stirred the entire time.

Thus (for all practical purposes), here I was again, alone. *Why isn't anyone else stirring?*

Going Home

I stopped to dip my sierra cup into the confines of Thielsen Creek for one last drink, taking a final look back toward the twenty-something campsite. But before I could move again, I was stopped by another thought.

I'm not like anyone else.

Over the course of the next few days, I trekked through Oregon's "Three Sisters" wilderness, named after the main peaks that towered over the area. The trail was easy to follow, having been etched firmly and deeply into a large plain, mostly by thousands of other day hikers.

Taking another drink from one of my water bottles, I moved to mop my sweaty brow. In short order a trail-section composed of obsidian came into view: a black glass-like rock base. The river that crossed the PCT at this point was clear and cold. The "deluxe-ness" of the area brought a smile to my face, as I envisioned Second-Time-Around coming through the area to yell "Deluxe!" a second time around. The weather was certainly perfect for such a scene.

I found myself contemplating why the weather had been so perfect for me since the start of the trek. Perhaps it was because of my many 'sacrifices' along the way, thus 'deserving' to be treated with such a sunny trail? *And of course: my honesty goes without saying,* I was quick to interject.

I took out a dried apple slice from my trail mix bag, and munched it slowly. It tasted like deception.

Exit wildflowers and obsidian. Enter volcanic rock and surrounding pumice. One sign well within the pumice read: "Water this way for hikers," and led to a man and his dog, at a camper-trailer on the shore of a lake.

"Hi," said the man, extending his hand. "Try this water."

I took the cup he offered me, and drank deeply. "From the lake?" I asked, pointing to the nearby reason for so many camper-trailers in one area.

"Oh, no, no, no," he said, laughing. "It's too polluted from everyone using it as a latrine and trash receptacle. This here that you got is from a spring down the road a piece. I bring it up especially for people like you. And by the way...," Trailer-Talker continued.

The conversation from his end went on and on. I certainly didn't feel like offending the jolly old man (especially after his gift of water), but I soon grew tired of so many words. "So where are you going to camp tonight?" he interjected.

It was near twilight. "I don't know."

"Nothing in the next fifteen miles," he continued. "Want to stay here? You could camp over here, or over there, or even over *there*, or even - "

"I'll go over there," I interrupted. "I get up early." The man laughed a hearty laugh while continuing a one-way conversation as I set up camp. Darkness approached, and he was still chattering. Even after entering my sleeping bag he kept rambling.

When I awoke the next morning, it took me nearly five minutes to recall what was going on. Packing quickly, and attaching a thank you note to the camper-trailer amidst deep buzzing of snores, I left.

CHAPTER 18: PASSING THROUGH WEDNESDAY, AUGUST 26, 1981 MILE 2062.2 AT THE OREGON / WASHINGTON STATE BORDER

Immediately after leaving Trailer-Talker's territory, there was a large volcanic field. Dipping to a low point, and then slowly ascending again as far as the eye could see, it seemed like another planet. The low point sported a yellow sign at a highway crossing.

The sun was just coming up over the flats, causing a variety of shiny effects off the volcanic rocks. The silence stood out profusely among brief whisps of the wind. *Last night's one-way conversation was sure a contrast.* I had plenty of Trailer-Talker's water, and would certainly need it.

Gradually ascending through the end of the volcanic field, Mount Washington beaconed in the distance, to the right. The guidebook indicated that numerous mountaineers attempt the peak, and therefore to not to be surprised if the only water-spring just off the side trail was dry.

(P.S. - It was)

A few days later I was hiking through another open volcanic field, and came upon a plateau at "Opple Dildock Pass." Across the northern landscape, I could see Mount Hood in the far distance. The end of Oregon was in sight!

The base of Mount Jefferson had its share of tourists. I saw the dots of people a long way off. Once descending into the valley near its base, I counted nearly sixty people in various clumps of civilized camping stalls. Groups of twos, threes, even sixes had congregated for God-knows-how-long and for God-knows-what. One two-some, approaching me from the other direction, stopped in front of me, and one of them asked me a question as I came to a halt.

"Are you a through-hiker?"

The other one turned. "What's a 'through-hiker'?" he asked.

"One passing through," I said, without thinking.

Strange looks came my way. "Through to what?"

Oh, brother... I mused. "Well, I'm hiking through on this trail to another trail."

Turning my attention to my legs, which were encased in dirt, I decided a short rinsing wouldn't hurt.

The reality was that I would be finishing soon, and I still had no place to call home.

Another road crossing. And another. A long ascent through trees.

At the lodge on the flank of Mount Hood, a sign signified mile number one thousand, eight hundred fifty two since Mexico, and four hundred, fifty two to go until Canada. The mileages were probably longer what with trail-additions since the sign was made, but eighteen hundred plus miles by foot, stamped on a sign in front of me, still made for an interesting sight.

My "pondering" was soon interrupted by voices: hundreds of them. The circus atmosphere suddenly became pronounced, and I became thirsty. Quickly turning and heading for the main door of the lodge, I was glad my backpack shielded me from the scuffling of others.

"Hey, Ash!"

I turned through the shuffling, in hopes of seeing the voice that knew my name. And there he was, all smiles.

"Hey, Flash!" I exclaimed back.

It was Wing Foot. And my, oh my, was it ever good to see him!

"Quite a sight, this Mount Hood, eh?" he said.

I stopped, and looked around. "Yeah, if I could see through all the people..."

"So, you want to team up?" he asked, ignoring the comment.

"Yeah, yeah, sure. For a while, anyway. But I think we'd better reevaluate our twosome when we hit Washington, just in case one of us drives the other batty."

My friend laughed heartily. "Washington state?" he exclaimed. "But that's only a couple of days away!" And then he added, "You *sure* you can handle me *that* long?"

Our last day in Oregon was much too long. We had decided to take the "PCT-alternate" route down Eagle Creek canyon, which was labeled 'more scenic' than the "official" PCT. Again, like the Crater Lake Rim Road, when a pathway was too heavily traveled by PCT standards, it was not stamped with PCT 'emblem-approval' along its length.

Wing Foot and I had hiked a number of miles before we even reached the head of the canyon. While looking over the number of miles remaining on the map, I noticed we would be pushing it to the limit by attempting to make the border of Washington state by the end of the day. I tried to discourage Wing Foot, but he wanted to go for it.

I looked at him, questioningly.

"My dad's there in a motel. We can join him tonight!" he exclaimed.

I looked down at my boots. "My feet are ready for a long break, Flash. Besides, we'll miss this area, going through it in the late afternoon and all." I was speaking of the views.

"Well, I'm going to go for it, Ash. You can decide for yourself."

Going Home

We passed various cascades of water in descending the canyon. There were times I felt like stopping for the day, but Wing Foot was determined to make town. When we reached 200-foot-high Tunnel Falls, the trail went literally through the rock bordering the footpath, in order to go underneath it (the wall of rock to one side was that steep). I was thankful for the thick cable-like railings that someone had forged into the rock wall along the trail.

My feet were killing me. I pondered taking off my boots, as I began to focus my camera in the twilight. Wing Foot suddenly spoke.

"Only a couple more miles, Ash!"

"Flash, are you SURE...?"

"Sure!" he exclaimed, taking off down the trail.

Finally exiting onto the trailhead parking lot, we stopped. It was well past twilight. "We could hike the two to three mile trail into town, Ash, OR we could hike the highway."

I turned, staring at him. For a very long instant I could not speak. "I didn't know it was that far into town," I finally said.

A pause. "Well, we can't camp here," Flash responded.

He was right. The ground was all pavement.

We hobbled our way east along Highway 84. The man-made lights were a significant help, even though they were encased in metal, horns, and fast-paced tires. We finally hit the town of Cascade Locks, Oregon, on the border of Washington state, at about 8 PM. Our tally that day was well over 32 miles since sunup.

We then turned to the motel. Once inside, Flash turned to his dad. I turned to the tub for my feet, and for the rest of me. How many pounds of trail dirt went down the drain on that one, I wasn't sure.

But I had made it through two states.

CHAPTER 19:
TOLL-BRIDGE FOR HIKERS

"So what?" asked Flash at breakfast the next morning. We were at the local diner. Flash's dad had gone to town to buy his son some extra supplies.

"But it's an accomplishment, don't you think?" I responded.

Wing Foot took off his cap, and then moved his fork to a nearby pile of scrambled eggs. He began to pile the mass into his mouth, while at the same time giving me the strangest look. "miffs," he muttered, through the eggs, "JmFst uh sefFcumdt." He swallowed hard, and then looked at me straight on.

"Ash, this trail is not the only thing that exists. There's more to life than what this hike holds. I was ready to quit at the end of California, you know."

"So why didn't you?"

The question caught my companion off guard. "Well, I - um - it - it just seemed like the thing to do, that's all!"

There's my opening, I thought. "Well, this 'thing,' as you put it," I started. "Why are we out here doing this anyway, in your opinion?

Flash paused, and took a sip of his coffee. "Because it's there. Why do you ask?"

"It - it's a life, wouldn't you say?" I asked.

Going Home

Flash laughed, almost spitting me with some coffee. "A – a what? Ash, this thing only lasts a few months, and then it's gone."

I cringed, and looked down at my plate. My toast was nearly ice-cold. "So - so you mean to tell me," I continued, after looking up at him again, "that you have it all planned out, when it's over?"

"Of course!"

"Well, if you don't mind me asking, what is that?"

Flash paused, and then gave me a very serious look. "I plan to form a backpacking company. The basis for my credentials will be having hiked the PCT."

"Hmmmmm…," I trailed off.

After a long silence, Wing Foot finally asked me, "So why is this thing so important to you?"

I paused. "I - I don't really know, Flash. It's got a hold of me, that's for sure. And I, unlike you, haven't the foggiest idea of what to do when it's all over."

"Hmmm. It looks like you need time to yourself again, Ash."

I excused myself to make a couple of phone calls. "I'll be right back," I told him.

"Collect call to Ashley Two State. Will you accept charges?" said the telephone operator.

"Uh, there's no one here by that name."

"Sir, would you like to speak to anyone else?"

"No thank you, Ma'am," I said, and hung up.

Quite a system for Mom, I thought, in order to save on phone charges. The call had cost nothing, yet she now knew exactly where I was.

"Collect call from Ashley. Will you accept charges?"

"Yes. Yes, I will!"

"Go ahead."

"Ash! Where ARE you? Did you make Washington yet?" asked Pro Verbs.

"Not yet," I responded. "But in about 100 paces I will be there."

"Wonderful! At this rate, you'll just keep hiking to Alaska!" she exclaimed.

I paused. "So how am I going to afford to get up there after I'm done hiking?"

"Don't worry," she continued. "I've already worked things out. You'll find details in a small box just inside Canada."

"Well, OK." *What's this noose?!* my mind screamed.

Flash and his dad were busy preparing for the day's activities when I went back to the motel to retrieve my things.

"I'm staying with my dad for a day or so Ash, so I'll just see you up the line."

"Right."

The first portion of the PCT that lead into Washington state was a man-made bridge designed for automobiles. It crossed the mighty Columbia River.

"Twenty-five cents, please," said the attendant as I came up to the toll booth.

"Huh?" I asked, not quite sure what he meant.

"We charge a twenty five cent toll to walk across this bridge," he said.

I frowned, and asked, "Why?"

"To pay for the bridge, I suppose."

I had just begun to enter into a conversation with the attendant on how many quarters it would take to pay for the bridge, when I heard a honk. Three cars were behind me, and the first obviously wanted to enter Washington state yesterday.

"How much do you charge them?" I asked.

"More than you," he responded.

"Well, OK. Here," I said, handing him a quarter. "It'll cut down on my weight, anyhow."

Going Home

I looked through the numerous openings in the bridge as I crossed. It made me nervous, for some reason. The heights had never scared me like this! At times the gaps in the bridge were so frequent that I thought I was walking on air. *Eyes straight ahead: don't look down!* I thought, as my pace quickly took hold. Once safely on the other side, I saw a larger sign just to the right in a car turnout. It read "Bridge of the Gods," and it had a paragraph of history attached. WHOSE gods? I questioned. *The god of quarters?!*

Well, at least I didn't have to ford the river...

CHAPTER 20: ASH TO ASHES

Pavement. Many cars going nowhere fast. These were some of my observations as I headed eastward toward the town of Stevenson on the "temporary PCT" from the bridge of the gods. By late morning, I had reached the main street. Upon entering, I noticed the sign: "ICE CREAM." I bought a ½ gallon (we had an ongoing PCT-club for this sort of thing).

It was late August. Summer tourist season was in full swing. People were moving slowly through the local shops as out-of-state cars crawled by. I stopped at one of the store fronts, and propped my pack up on the bench next to me.

The sky started clouding over. I hurriedly finished my ice cream, and then stooped down to shoulder my pack, then east along the street's shoulder. A mile or so down the road at the next juncture, the "PCT" turned north, running into the permanent trail in short order.

The clouds began to rain a fine mist. This was the first airborne water that I had encountered along the entire trail – well actually, the second – the first being the sprinklers of the Mojave City Park many weeks back. I took out my rain suit and put it on.

It felt funny: too confining.

One half-hour later, I was drenched in a combination of mist and sweat. *I thought this Goretex was supposed to work!*

Going Home

I bellowed inside of my head. (Later, I would be informed that the suit I took was first-generation material: the "bugs" were not worked out of it.) My consolation, however, was this: the plastic covering my pack was not first-generation Goretex.

I finally reached the first section of "real" Washington-state PCT. "Ah, trail!" I exclaimed. Joy, however, soon turned to frustration, as the freshly-cut footpath exhibited numerous tree stumps and roots. In addition, the first switchbacks were haphazard, erratically sloped.

"Welcome to Washington!" I exclaimed, to no one in particular.

The next three days passed slowly, complete with 100% mist. My equipment seemed much heavier. Whether it was I really did not know. But everything was wet, that I knew! Thus, a new obstacle came into being: 'Extra Time To Repack Things Come Morning.'

The fourth day, the mist stopped. But the clouds remained.

Mount Saint Helens came into view that fourth day through a group of trees. There had been many warnings based on the May 1980 eruption, indicating closure without delay if another eruption seemed imminent. In the back of my mind had been a 'Plan B:' to hike around the area of concern to White Pass, in case this happened. But thankfully, I did not have to hike all those extra road miles.

Through the gray clouds over the mountain, I could see steam rising from Mount Saint Helens' strangely-shaped summit. Then I looked down, and noticed the trail itself. Stooping down to get a closer look, I picked up some of the sandy pathway in my hand and rubbed it together between my fingers. It was ash from the mountain: not the usual trail bed. But it was much coarser than the stuff I had seen in gift shops back south, due in part to gravity holding the heavier stuff closer to the mountain. After a short standing break,

Going Home

I slowly shuffled forward on the PCT through the sandy mass.

I saw no one through this section.

In time, I came to the base of Mount Adams. The PCT in this section skirted around its western flank. The sun came through the fast-moving clouds at irregular intervals, and I realized how much I missed it being there all the time. The air was cooler now than in Oregon, and the sun did little to warm my body.

I stopped during one break to sit by a glacial-melt stream coming off the mountain. Its color was like grayish milk, and added to the damp atmosphere. It certainly didn't look too inviting to drink! For a split-second I thought about filtering some of it through a bandanna to drink, but then immediately dismissed the idea. For not only had I tried this before, but this time it looked more like liquid dirt!

Where is everyone else? I pondered, in crossing the stream. I started humming the theme song from an upbeat movie, ..., when it happened.

The trail disappeared.

I had seen this type of situation before. Stream crossings had never posed much of a problem in the California-section of the PCT, but there the similarity ceased. I could not put my finger on it, but here the stream crossing seemed - different. I found myself staring at my wet feet, with my boots still tied around my neck, after crossing the milky-gray glacial stream. It took a while in the crisp fall air to dry my feet before I could don the boots again.

The trail then reappeared as I continued hiking. It was simply hidden beneath the ash that blended the sidelines.

In the days that followed, I was thrust into more sunshine. It felt good. Rain-washed ash, now multi-colored in artistic swirls, filled vast portions of the trail. I hated walking across the paintings, but it was the only way through. Birds were chirping distinctly as I strolled along.

I had just started humming a tune, when I heard the crunching of familiar boots behind me.

"Ash!"

"Yes, it is!" I exclaimed. "All over the place!!"

"You done being solo, for the time being?" a Wing-footed question replied.

I looked beyond him. "So where's Second-Time-Around?"

Flash shifted his backpack atop his slender legs. "Haven't the foggiest. Anyway, what do you think? You want company?"

I nodded my head.

"Well, good. I need someone to talk to. This trail gets lonely, and I can't wait to get home."

"But what about all these wonderful views?" I questioned.

"Views are fine," my friend responded, "but this trail's been too long. I want to get started on my new backpacking company."

As we trekked, we found ourselves steadily rising in elevation. The PCT snaked its way around various no-name canyons before emerging upon a long boulder field. At the end of the field was a shelter, and it was there that we stopped.

Flash took out his water bottle, while noting the snow pack, and took a deep drink. I took out the guidebook and started to read. "The guidebook says right here that this shelter sits above 7,000 feet. It's named for a twelve-year-old girl who lost her life."

Flash nearly choked on his water. "Up HERE?"

I kept reading. "Well, it doesn't say how she died. But it does say that we can camp inside the shelter if we want."

It was true that the day was not yet over, and we could have easily hiked a few more miles. Yet this shelter, and the surrounding area (with views of Mount Saint Helens and Mount Adams, as well as Mount Rainier) had a unique and pristine quality about it. Flash and I exchanged glances, wondering whether or not to stop for the day.

Case closed.

CHAPTER 21: HUCKLEBERRY HIKER

Wing Foot awoke. He came out of the shelter and began to read me the guidebook. The accompanying trail description just ahead of us stopped him from reading. "Hey, Ash," he said, handing me the book. "Look at this."

I started to read the first few paragraphs. The storyline described the area in sweeping superlatives, and then went into an Indian legend about the three mountains of Adams, Saint Helens and Rainier, and how they related to one another in a 'personal way.'

I was not too impressed. "I'd rather they just cut the ghost stories," I stated, handing him back the book.

"Well, sure," he responded, "but at least it keeps us from getting lost!"

Of course, he was right.

It took a while with ice-cold hands to pack our belongings before we headed out. Our wide-eyed stares toward each other gave way to an interesting trail dance. Flash was the first one to speak.

"Man," he said, taking off his boots, "I feel like I'm part of that Indian legend the trailguide talked about, what with this dancing and all!"

After a bit of awkward silence, I asked, "So, how do we warm these things up? Sleep with them next time?!"

Flash's response was immediate. "Vancouver, here we come!"

We made our way slowly across the highest point of the Washington state PCT, along the top of Packwood Glacier. In surveying the crossing however, we did see footprints of some previous boots: *other through-hikers*, we wondered?

"Where's the goats, Ash?" Flash had just stopped and turned around to ask me the question.

My response was quick, as I wanted to get across this ice field now. "Not here. Keep moving."

Once we finally made it across the glacier, we stopped to take a break. Our boots were sufficiently thawed from the heat of our feet, but in removing mine I noticed very moist socks and shriveled feet. Ahead, I could see the trail traversing the knife-edged ridgeline as a true crest trail.

"Deluxe," I said.

"Huh?"

"Second Time Around," I added.

"Hey, Ash?" he interjected.

"What?"

A pause. "Where's the elk?"

I didn't know if he was kidding, or what. But we were near Elk Pass.

Signs indicated we would have had to back up more than 1,000 trail feet if we met a mule or horse pack train coming the other direction, since the PCT dropped off steeply on both sides. My nerves and muscles were fully strung as Wing Foot spoke.

"I was wondering, Ash."

I stopped, and slowly turned to face him. "Yeah, what?"

"Where's the horses and mules? I don't see any wildlife."

He, haw, I thought. "Forget the wildlife," I snorted.

The trail finally began to descend and meander through some very lush meadows. Flash took the lead, and I found it more and more difficult to carry on any sort of a conversation, talking through his backpack (which muffled most of my words). Trying to lean around his pack when speaking proved to be a fiasco also, as my hiking rhythm went helter-skelter.

So we continued walking, in silence.

White Pass: ski resort. First highway crossing on the Washington-state PCT. One of the only places in southern Washington where one could resupply, via trucks from the east – once a day.

I had one box and one letter waiting. The box was full of the usual goodies, and had a checkered array of postal stamps from central Alaska. Once I had finished repacking my pack, the letter was opened. "Welcome to Washington, Ash!" it said, in San Diego tones.

I separated from Wing Foot just after White Pass. (He needed a short layover more than going home, and I didn't.) And here I was, in the middle of shrubbery thoroughly obscuring the trail. Their colorfully bushy leaves housed numerous berries, and I started to look at them. Pulling out my little berry-finder booklet, which had been mailed to me in the White Pass parcel, I began to key in berry types.

I had heard about berry poisonings before, and did not want to take any chances here.

Let's see, I thought. *Leaf - this shape ... this many leaves per bush ... this type of -* Five long minutes passed before I finally remembered to remove the pack from my back: so intense was my concentration. Time seemed to stand still, as I checked the booklet again and again.

Suddenly, an unknown hiker came out of nowhere and grabbed a handful of berries from a nearby bush. He then stuffed them into his mouth, and exclaimed through the juice, "Man, I love these huckleberries, don't you?"

Great...

Going Home

The trail appeared shortly. I would stop every once in a while to enjoy the free berry feast, and through the juice tried my best to ward off the emotions that told me I would be finishing soon.

My thoughts shifted to God, to Maps Man, and to Pro Verbs. And through all the shifting, one question kept nagging me.

Why am I hiking so hard?

CHAPTER 22:
TOO SHORT, TOO LONG
WEDNESDAY,
SEPTEMBER 9, 1981
MILE 2260.5 AT SNOQUALMIE
PASS, WASHINGTON

A final plateau and view of a great heron led me to Snoqualmie Pass ski resort, the halfway point along the Washington-state section of the PCT. It was only the second PCT highway crossing in the entire state of Washington.

I was well ahead of schedule in arriving: almost two weeks! But in calculating this "schedule" from the beginning of the trek, I had neglected to provide Pro Verbs with the latest revisions along the way.

Thus, my supplies were not here.

There were other through-hikers here on layover. They didn't seem too concerned about anything, whereas I in turn felt anxious about everything. I had checked-in at the Post Office noting the distinct absence of any of my packages.

"When do you get your mail tomorrow?" I asked the postal clerk.

"Depends, sonny. Might be mid-afternoon before the truck gets here."

Oh, great. What to do? I had enough left in my backpack to make Stevens Pass (the next resupply point a few days north) it was true, but deep down inside I feared I might be missing something.

"Don't you want to sign the trail register?" the clerk continued.

I paused. "Can you forward my package when it gets here?" I interjected, taking the pen.

"For a price," she replied.

I was number 12 in the trail register. No-Time, for example, had long since passed through. His only comment in passing was "Where's the views?" I asked the clerk just how many more hikers she expected to come through this time of the year.

"Not many. Snows'll probably be here soon."

That would mean whoever was behind me might reach an impasse.

Boom, boom, boom. I headed northward, almost "sprint-walking" past some day-hikers coming from the PCT at the Snoqualmie Pass highway crossing. I was breathing heavily as I climbed.

I camped just beyond a ridge, and left before dawn the next day.

Miles, miles, miles. I was so set on pace-walking, this second day out from Snoqualmie Pass that I nearly stepped on a porcupine crossing the trail in the late afternoon. That stopped me.

But only briefly.

I camped at Spectacle Lake that night. It truly was a spectacle. But I left it behind before the next day's sun ever creased it.

Miles, miles, and more miles. Even though I found specks of time to take photos, my emotions were super-charged. In essence, I was channeling all my impatience, all my boredom and all my energies into pace walking, to try to keep from thinking too much. But I was unable to quell the rising excitement and strange sense of loss within me. *I need to miss the snows up ahead, but - then – it'll all be through!*

That night I dreamed someone was following me, hiking at least as fast as I was. I woke up before he caught me in my dream.

Going Home

This was the first time on the trek that I had found myself breathing heavily in my sleep.

Road crossing: Stevens Pass ski resort. No Post Office: only a ranger station that graciously held parcels for through-hikers. Two boxes were here for me: the one forwarded from Snoqualmie Pass, and the "next one" from Alaska. The combined volume of both probably surpassed that of a small refrigerator.

The ranger looked at me smugly. "So wha'cha gonna do with all this-here stuff? Hire a donkey or something?"

The statement caught me off guard, but he did have a point.

"Can I mail one of the boxes back from here?" I asked.

"For a price," the ranger drawled. "And as long as it's sealed properly."

I had no packing tape. And one box of supplies was all I could carry.

"Take this one here," I said, pointing to the one forwarded from Snoqualmie Pass. (Correspondence contained inside would have to wait.)

I then turned my attention to the other parcel. Once transferred to my pack, I noted there was still time to make a few miles before sunset. And so I went.

The weather was warm for late-September. I felt strong, even though my hips still hurt at the waist, and my knees were giving me some minor problems. The balls of my feet were so callused from all the hundreds of miles of hiking that circulation was being cut off to my toes.

Four days north of Stevens Pass, I became engulfed in fog.

As I walked, I listened for rustling in the bushes or whisping through the trees in order to get my bearings. But all I heard was the methodical shush-shush-shushing of my boots through the damp ash deposited by Mount Saint Helens along the trail.

Going Home

I stopped and listened. The silence was stifling, and intense. Soon I reached a trail junction, which was without a sign.

For some reason, the choking silence intensified further. I became cognizant of fear sweeping over my limbs. The more heavily-traveled pathway went to the left. So I left my pack at the signless junction and walked up to the left for a few hundred yards. (Map and compass were useless here, as I couldn't see anything through the dense fog) Returning to the junction, I threw up my hands. After ten more minutes, I finally decided to take the path less traveled.

Robert Frost would have loved this. It proved to be the right path.

I met two "four-day" hikers a few days later, and joined them at their request. Jovial Jokester and Commissioned Counterpart proved to be a great encouragement for me. They jested with each other constantly, and even kidded me for staying out on the trail for too long.

A few miles south of south of Rainy Pass (the last highway crossing in Washington state), we were spread out of sight from one another. I was in the middle. Rounding a corner, I spotted a rustling in the nearby bushes. I stopped, and then moved closer to investigate. The rustling abruptly ceased as I came within a few yards of the main bush. Suddenly, up popped a furry head.

It was a mama bear! Slowly, I began to walk backwards up the trail, ice-axe 'chinked' into position (as if that would have helped). Rounding the first corner, I turned and ran at Feather River pace back to Commissioned Counterpart.

We both walked back slowly to the corner where I had spotted the bear. Ever so carefully, I peeked around the corner, and then (finally) over the 'bear bush.' After a few tense seconds, off in the distance, I noted the mama bear and her cub limbering the other direction. I breathed a heavy sigh of relief.

Going Home

We trekked ahead, and finally reached Jovial Jokester, who was resting at a stream.

"A bear? What bear?" he asked.

"You - you walked right *by* him, I mean her, I mean them!" I stammered. "How'd you - ever - "

"Ash, I think it's time for you to quit," JJ interjected. "You've been out here on this trail far too long."

CC just laughed as I threw my visor at him.

We finally reached Rainy Pass amidst rainy mist and purple Fireweed flowers. Sun-streaked cloud formations interspersed the sky just behind us. The air was quite crisp now: a clear indication that winter was just around the corner. Here at the pass, there was no ski resort or place to resupply. But there was the same VW Bus I had seen back in Cascade Locks, just across the highway in a parking lot, and just outside it a familiar dad of a familiar through-hiker. Before I could speak, the familiar through-hiker poked his head out the side door of the bus.

"Only a few more days, Ash!"

Flashy Wing Foot jumped out of the van, and we embraced.

"Flash, I'd like for you to meet - "

But as I turned, CC and JJ had disappeared.

Then a car drove up. "We were just leaving," Commissioned Counterpart said. "We've got to get back to Seattle."

"You keep hiking strong, y'hear?" Jovial Jokester exclaimed from the car. "Then quit this trail for good! You've been out here too long!"

"My sentiments exactly!" responded my partner.

I could only roll my eyes.

CHAPTER 23:
OH CANADA
SATURDAY, SEPTEMBER 26, 1981 MILE 2,452.3 AT MANNING PARK, CANADA

Flash took quite a bit of extra time with his dad, even after the departure of the JJ and CC. Finally bidding his dad adieu, Flash walked up to me with that same dinosaur-sized pack atop those same matchstick legs. His walk was slow and his demeanor was subdued. I had decided to wait at the parking lot restroom for him so he could say goodbye to his dad.

I looked up at him as he stopped. Then I asked, "So - how's dad?"

"Ah, you know. Hated to leave. But he's not cut out to walk this type of thing: even the last miles, though he wanted to. So I'll catch him at the end."

I started to say something, but Flash interjected. "C'mon. Let's get going." Then he marched away from the restroom without another word.

That night, we camped only a few miles north of Rainy Pass, near a plateau-like ridge that overlooked a basin. We spent more time than usual setting up camp, since the air was very cold. Gloves proved to be much too cumbersome for the delicate art of untying knots. *Just like in the Boy Scouts,* I mused, in-between rubbing my hands.

All night long, I heard the off-and-on pitter-patter of snow dusting my tent.

In the morning, I unzipped the tent door just enough to see what lay outside. Three inches of newly fallen snow now covered everything. It was beautiful! But my partner was standing outside of *his* tent, hands in pockets, shivering in the early morning light.

He heard my rustling. "Time to fly, Ash!" he yelled, in-between jumps.

I looked beyond him, still wrapped in my sleeping bag. "But this sunrise!" I exclaimed. "Just look at that reddish hue!"

"I don't care about the hue view, Ash," Wing Foot replied, stamping his feet. "I just want to get started!"

I paused. "I'm already started on my second dream," I said, from the warmth of my bag.

I got a faceful of snow.

That day we trekked through Harts Pass, 35 miles from the USA/Canada border.

"You got your entry permit, Ash?"

"Right here."

"And all your notes?" He had watched me journaling off and on since first meeting me. "Well, most are mailed back home, you know," I responded.

"I'm not surprised," Wing Foot said. "What with all those notes, you could probably write your own trailguide!"

"Well, I may write a book."

"So's everyone else, Ash."

Yeah, right.

The border came into view as we crested a ridgeline on a plateau. The weather had an ever-increasing sharp bite to it: the kind that made your sweat run cold the moment it comes through your pores. Gloves, stocking hat, and ankle-topped gaiters were the norm now.

"By the looks of things, Flash," I stated, "we'd better get out of here in the next couple days. By then it'll be winter."

He nodded.

Going Home

"Where's your wing-footed hat?" I asked him.

"I left it with my dad at Rainy Pass. Didn't you notice?"

I hadn't noticed. "So - so what am I supposed to call you now?"

He paused. "Call me 'Going Home'."

Hopkins Lake was typically the final camping ground for south-to-north through-hikers, seven miles from Canada. We bypassed it though, in order to camp right on the border itself. It reminded me of our last day in Oregon state, as we bypassed everything in order to get to a motel, but there was one difference now.

One of us was Going Home.

"It's a THERE!" I exclaimed, as the USA/Canada border appeared just in front of us.

In a flash, I nearly got run over by my hiking companion, who was now heading the other way on winged feet. It took a second or two to regain my composure before stripping off my backpack and in turn running after him. I caught him near the second bend.

"Where in the world are YOU going?!" I yelled.

"Out of here!!" came the response.

"But why?!!" I yelled, even louder, as Going Home kept running away from going home.

He stopped, and turned briefly to face me, breathing heavily. "To get away from the bear! YOU'RE the one who just spotted him!"

The next morning we decided to take pictures of each other crossing the border. "So who's first?" I asked.

Going Home frowned. "What does it matter?" he asked.

I paused for effect. "Because," I continued, "whoever goes over first to take a picture of the other will in their photo be actually crossing the border for the second time."

A distinct cringe. "The things you think of, Ash!"

But out of those photos, the cover of this book was born. I distinctly remembered leaning into the sun when Going Home took the picture.

We stowed our cameras. "You ready?" I was asked.

"For what?" I asked back.

"To go home!"

"Well, maybe for you…"

My partner stared at me for a long instant. "What's *that* supposed to mean?"

There was another pause, but shorter. "I'm not ready yet."

Going Home leaned on a nearby post as he formulated his words. "Oh come on, Ash, get with it! The trail's over. It's time to go home!"

"You don't want to camp out here another night?"

Going Home looked at me in a strange way. "Looks like you need to be by yourself again, Ash," he said.

I nodded, and put my pack down.

And then he was gone.

CHAPTER 24: AFTERMATH

I stopped only three miles into Canada at Windy Joe Campground. Removing my backpack at one of the center campsites, I slowly stabilized it against a rock in the upright position. It was true that I had accomplished what I had set out to do: hiking the entire length of the Pacific Crest Trail from Mexico to Canada. But amazingly, I felt no emotions of ecstasy or jubilance now that the finish line was crossed.

It was still well before noon. Spotting a nearby stump, I sat down and tried to pray. It was something I heard about during childhood. The mountains never talked to me in a way that made sense beyond a trial existence, anyway. But I was unable to concentrate on anything at all, so I gave it up.

I sacked out well before sunset, and tried to sleep. It was a long and lonely night.

In the morning I got up quickly. I made the final four miles hiking in well under two hours. Upon entering the PCT registration office, I signed the register, and noted less than a dozen other names of accomplished through-hikers for 1981. For example, No-Time had made it in just over four months, commenting, "Why so much fog? I missed all the views..." I added my own comments, which came out dry and void of life. The main lodge of Manning Provincial Park was next, to purchase a greyhound bus ticket for Vancouver.

Going Home

I stared out of the window of the bus, now ten miles west of the PCT terminus. I thought of all the heights and depths I had conquered. *How would this compare to the trail of life up ahead?* I thought of the fact that I was one of the few who had finished. *Would this add polish to my resume?* I thought of my family in Michigan, who I would be visiting soon. *How would I be greeted upon arrival?* I thought of Maps Man, Wild Bill, and others back south. *Would I ever see them again?* And I thought of Pro Verbs. *What awaited me in Alaska, after my side-trip to Michigan?* I then thought of the strange emptiness which kept gripping my insides. *Why hadn't the PCT fulfilled me?* Finally, I thought of God. *Where is He, in all of this?*

I leaned back, and tried to relax.

My cousin, her husband, and their little girl met me at the Vancouver, B.C. bus terminal, and after many hugs and smiles took me to their Canadian home. Enroute, we stopped to drop off my final two rolls of film for over-night professional developing.

"My, my, my. Look at your boots!" exclaimed my cousin, upon exiting from the car. "They look so much different than our little one's booties!" (and) "My, oh my!" her husband interjected. "That's quite a load you've got there," she stated, as I was removing my backpack from the trunk of their car. "Looks like you got good use out of it!"

I managed a weak smile.

"This photo here," began the developer, "is an impossible picture."

It was mid-afternoon the next day.

"What do you mean?" I asked.

Designed Developer moved to project the slide in question onto a screen.

"The light coming to your head," he began, "has more than one line on it. That's pretty weird. But then it stops at your head, and shows no shadow of corresponding length behind your feet."

I moved closer to the screen. *Yes, this was odd: that's for sure.* "What else?" I finally asked.

"Well," DD drawled, scratching his chin. "There's just no way the light could have reflected off the camera lens, in order to make such an imprint of light on the film, since the sun is shining from BEHIND the camera." He paused, while I continued to stare at the screen. "Did you touch this up in any way before you brought these rolls of film in to me yesterday?"

A flush of emotion ran over me: like the kind you get when you sense someone is watching you and you know you're not guilty. "No," I said. "I mean, how could I? I swear, I brought them here right after I took them!"

He paused, and scratched his chin again. "Well, I knew that," he said. "I've been at this for quite a few years, and frankly I don't see any evidence of touch-up or alteration of the film. But I had to ask." Designed Developer's voice was firm. "I must say, though, that this slide would make one heck of a cover for a book some day."

I pondered his statement. "So where was it taken?" he asked.

"Near the end, at the border," I said. "How much do I owe you?"

"It's paid for. Someone already took care of it."

I flew into Michigan two days later. Banners, balloons, and smiles greeted me as I walked through the terminal gate. Everyone looked so proud of me. I could feel my head swelling. "He just got done walking 2,500 miles!" I heard someone say, as a beer was sloshed my way. But all I really remember is the blank look on the bartender's face.

On October 13, 1981, the Western Michigan Poison Control Center had a special thank-you celebration regarding my completion of the PCT hike and corresponding walk-a-thon for them. Two days later, I was asked to appear with the head of the center on TV for an interview. I went to it in the exact same wool shirt that I took with me on the trail.

My mom washed it first, though.

"Many donations for the Poison Center have come in as a result of the publicity (on the TV) and the Editorial (in the newspaper)," Center Head explained after the interview. "Also, County DHS has granted us $10,000 from their Discretionary Funds and they have stated that they are willing to help us try to obtain more money from the other counties which we serve. As a result of that Editorial we have had many more calls and checks sent to us. At a recent Sub-Committee Meeting of our Board of Trustees, it was decided to recommend to the full Board that our hospital attract a full-time fund raiser for purposes such as the Poison Center and several other programs at the hospital."

I should be happy, I thought.

In late October of 1981, just one month after the USA/Canadian PCT border crossing, I arrived in Alaska. There were no igloos in sight as I stepped off the plane, thankfully.

Pro Verbs was elated, bubbling with excitement. She wrapped her arms tightly around my neck for what seemed like an eternity. I soon had trouble breathing.

When I was able to pry her arms off me to catch my breath, I asked her, "So why is everything so - so *brown* here?"

"Oh, it's still fall-time, silly," she giggled. "Just wait a couple of weeks, and you'll see the colors change."

Soon we were on the highway north from Anchorage. Pro Verbs was speaking about all different types of things as we bounded up the road. "Check this radio station out, Ash," she interjected. "They don't play the same song twice in a week. It's great!"

I rolled down the window. Some air would be nice.

Her car finally came to a halt in a small gravel parking lot, and I looked out the windshield at the building in front of me. "Is this it?" I quipped.

"Oh, you'll learn to love it," she countered. "It's really quite a quaint place, once you get to know it."

Quaint...

"Come on," she said, unlocking the door. "Bring your backpack on up and I'll give you the grand tour."

The first thing that stood out to me once I entered the building was all the PCT equipment stuffed in a back room. I gasped. "That's all mine?!"

She laughed. "Sure! What did you expect?"

I looked around the room. Dried food lay everywhere in neat little stacks, as if someone was planning a hike.

My hands moved to a small hole in the wall. "What's this newspaper doing in here?"

"Insulation," she said, not skipping a beat. "These places used to be used for barracks for the guys that worked on the pipeline back in the mid-70's. The construction crew kind of skimped on a few things."

"Do you have a newspaper here?"

She stopped, and looked at me strangely. "Whatever for?"

"I'd like to look for a job."

Pro Verbs cocked her head. "My goodness, Ash, you just got here!"

"I know," I said, ignoring the tenor of her statement, "but it's been so long that I held a job, I think I need to bone up."

The next morning over coffee, I stated, "Here's a job I can hike to." I was pointing at the paper in the middle of the classifieds. "The maps you left out indicate it's only a couple of miles cross-country as the crow flies. I went ahead and set up the interview while you were in the shower."

Pro Verbs gave me another quizzical look. "But Ash," she responded, "the country's quite a bit different up here than down in the lower 48."

I put down the paper, and jerked my head. "But - but I just finished hiking across all *kinds* of country!" I exclaimed.

She shrugged. "It's not like back where you came from, Ash," she went on to say. "Some of the places out here have never been hiked. Very few trails, too."

What does SHE know? I'm an experienced hiker! I shouted in my mind.

I rose, and left in a huff.

Four hours later, I stumbled into the building where my interview would be held, drenched from the waist down. I had fallen into two creeks enroute. "Wha- what time is it?" I asked, in exasperation.

The receptionist took one long look at me, and then asked, "What happened to YOU?"

I rubbed my hands together. "Can we set up another interview?" I asked, in response.

I spent a while drying out my pants and socks there, courtesy of a space heater located in the restroom. Both my legs and my pride were smarting. I finally decided to hike back to the apartment on paved roads, the long way around. This would hopefully give me time to think without worrying about any more 'Alaskan surprises.'

What was going on? I wondered, as my boots shuck, shuck, shucked along the pavement. *What is happening to me?!*

I sat down by the side of the road. There were no cars in sight. The air was cold, and everything was still.

But still, someone was trying to get my attention.

CHAPTER 25: EPILOGUE
WEDNESDAY, JUNE 1, 1983
MILE 0.0 AT CHURCH IN THE WILDWOOD, ALASKA

"Insight is a breakthrough, requiring much intellectual dismantling and dislocation. It begins with a mental interim, with a culmination of a feeling for the unfamiliar, unparalleled, incredible. It is in being involved with a phenomenon, being intimately engaged to it, courting it, as it were, that after much perplexity and embarrassment we came upon insight - upon a way of seeing the phenomenon from within. Insight is accompanied by a sense of surprise. What has been closed is suddenly disclosed. It entails genuine perception, seeing anew. We who think that we can see the same object twice have never seen. Paradoxically, insight is knowledge at first sight."
(from "the Prophets," as given in the bibliography)

The sun was setting. I had just finished another day in a "normal" (Alaskan) living environment. It was the spring of 1982.

The past few months of adjustment had left me longing for another lifestyle. *This life – surrounding Alaska – is not like home...*

I was jarred out of my thoughts by a question.

Going Home

"So how come you're not interested in hiking anymore?" Pro Verbs asked.

I shook my head. "Why do you say that?" I asked.

"Because you've stored nearly all your equipment away right after you got here, and haven't touched it since. I just don't get it. You were so gung-ho on hiking."

"Well, that's because then it had a purpose," I replied.

"A what?"

"A purpose. You know, a vision. That which gets you through the hard spots."

"But Ash," she said, "That was then. Can't you backpack just for fun now?"

She didn't understand, I could see that.

"I need to go for a walk," I said.

I went to the spare bedroom, and stole a long glance into the closet where I had stored my PCT equipment. I then reached out, and touched the backpack which had been my faithful 'house-companion' for nearly half of 1981.

It's much better to return, I thought, but I deep down inside I knew that I could not.

I grabbed the little bible I had taken on the PCT-hike, and went strolling out the driveway to the apartment complex, and then up the road. One thing about Alaska (away from the big city of Anchorage) was that usually very few cars were out and about. Nice for solitude.

I had just rounded a bend in the road, when I stopped.

What am I doing - ? I asked.

No one answered.

I sat down on the side of the road. It was hard to go on. (My sister in Michigan knew that. And so she kept praying.)

I then turned to a memory of long ago – those twelve husky fishermen on the wall – and remembered only one name: that of my dad, John. Reflexively, I opened the little bible to the end of the book by the same name, and began to read.

"Most assuredly, I say unto you: when you were young, you girded yourself, and walked where you wished. But when you are old, you will stretch forth your hands, and another will gird you, and carry you where you do not wish to go."

I didn't know if my dad, or someone else, was speaking to me. Or if it was for someone else.

It was the winter of 1982. Months of Alaska were now under my feet. I had re-entered society (so to speak) by making a fair amount of money, courtesy of the Alaskan Fish and Game industry. This summertime job deposited a check into my account each month while I was out tagging fish in Alaska's west-central "bush" community. Pro Verbs, having a pretty good job herself, had managed to secure a house in the beautiful Matanuska Valley area a few miles north of Anchorage, and here we were: moving in stereo, TV, VCR, this and that: every-thing from my "to-be-happy" list of long ago. The house would be ready to occupy in another few months. Cut-up wood, courtesy of a bulldozed area and a chainsaw, now filled an area between two live trees in the backyard. Our driveway was complete with two cars: paid for.

Yet as I visited day after day to note the house, something wasn't quite right. I entered the front door, and sat down on the couch to watch some TV.

But this day I didn't turn it on.

The sun was shining at low flanks into the south-facing living room window. I found myself thinking of the trail.

It was a very pretty environment, this. Real Estate projections placed this domicile as tripling in value in only a year. So I should be happy.

Help, I cried to no one in particular.

* * * * *

Going Home

"May I help you?"

I was the spring of 1983. I had just answered a knock at the apartment door. Pro Verbs was at work, and I was home, waiting for my next part-time working assignment.

"Would you like a book that helps to explain the Trailguide?" someone asked.

I didn't know what to say.

"You *do* have a Trailguide, don't you?" he asked.

Before I could stop staring, he continued. "This book, with pictures and amplifications, will help explain the Trailguide. It's free for the taking."

I reached out and took the 'Your Trailguide And You' book from him. I slowly began to thumb through it. It had a lot of chapters. Then looking up, I started to ask him a question.

But he was gone.

I looked outside. No car was there. *Hmmm,* I thought.

I closed the front door, and went to the couch. I opened the book and read for a few minutes. Something began to click. My mind kept countering with, *But there's not even a backpack or trail in these pictures!*

I got up to make coffee. 'Your Trailguide And You' had made references to the Bible, a book I had despised in my teenage years, and a book I had taken with me on the PCT for purposes of 'non-reading security.' Upon returning to the couch with my coffee, a thought struck me. I began to sense that there was more than a long-distance hike involved in this "Trailguide."

All of a sudden, an intense stillness filled the room. It had been quiet before, but *this* quiet was consuming, and yet not stifling. I began to speak to the air.

"If - if You're really real," I began, stuttering, "theh - then please show me who - the Trailguide is - You are. I - " Looking down at my coffee, I closed with, "I'm just tired of walking - by myself..."

"And so we return home: to family, to community, to the needs of the city. But the wilderness abides, and we will return here some-day as well. We think of biblical wilderness as an arena to pass through only once. But Jesus returned. The prophets returned. Hosea would have had the entire nation return. Someday in the future we will return. To gather our spiritual bearings, to grow in the silence and solitude, to feel the contours of fear and grace. And to recall who is God and who we are and what God would have us to do."

(from the book entitled "Wilderness Sojourn," as given in the bibliography)

Memorial Day Weekend, 1983. 'Your Trailguide And You' continued to weigh heavily on my mind, and I would refer to it often. But I really didn't know where to begin to search for the Trail that the book spoke about.

I decided to go to the Yellow Pages. The church I had grown up with, including 12 husky fishermen on the walls, would probably be found under "Churches," I thought. But even if not, the search might prove to be interesting.

"Hello?"

"Hello. Can you tell me about the Guide?" I asked, on my first phone call.

Silence.

"Hello?" I asked.

"Um, well," a voice began, "We - we, uh, open the building at nine and eleven on Sunday mornings. You would be more than welcome to come."

"Huh?" I said.

"Do you need to know how to get here?"

Oh, brother. Next number, please.

"Hello?"

"Hello. Can you tell me about the Guide?"

"I beg your pardon?" came the reply.

"The Guide. What can you tell me about Him?"

A pause. "Let me let you talk to my wife."

Going Home

I hung up before she got to the phone. Time to dial again.

"Hello?"

"Hello. What can you tell me about the Guide?"

A pause. "Second Timothy Three Sixteen," came the thoughtful reply.

"What was that?" I questioned.

"It's in the Trailguide. It will help you get started on your journey," he said, and hung up.

Odd, I thought. But then I remembered the little bible I had taken with me, in my backpack, on the PCT, two years prior.

I went to the desk where I had stashed it, and opened the bottom drawer. Yes, there it was: just as I had placed it. Turning it over and over in my hand, my mind began to roam. On the PCT hike, it had seemed almost a nuisance, taking up space and weight, while all the while forming a false sense of security within me. But now here, after all these months, it was now beckoning to be read.

I opened the book of Second Timothy, which I found in the Table of Contents. Then I found Chapter Three, followed by Verse Sixteen. Slowly I read the first few words. *What was that?*

I asked. I then turned to the copyright page, and read about some new king named James. Then I went back to those same few words, and read them aloud. My eyes opened wide.

It was time to plan. Someone had spoken, and Pro Verbs would be home soon.

"Ash, you look like you're planning for some type of hike."

Pro Verbs statement was perceptive. So I responded in like manner.

"Well, I am. It's a bit different kind of hike, though. I've already seen a few of the valleys in the planning, so to speak, and now I'm ready for the heights." I held up the Yellow Pages, open to "Churches," for her to see.

She looked at me strangely. "Ever since I've known you, Ash," she started, "you've stayed clear from this type of thing. What gives?"

"Well," I replied, "that's what this 'Avoid' list is for."

She looked at it, half-interested. "So what are those OTHER papers for?" she asked, pointing to the table full of maps and diagrams.

"Diversions and side-trips," I said.

She rolled her eyes, and then looked at me, almost jeering.

"My goodness Ash, can't you settle down? Even since you came to Alaska, you haven't been the same."

"Well, ever since I got here," I responded, "I've wondered about you, too. Don't you ever think about what's beyond the PCT?" I asked, holding up the Yellow Pages again.

She frowned, and then threw up her hands. "I tried that once, Ash. You couldn't get me to go back to one of those places," she responded, rather distantly.

I stood up from my chair. "But that - that was the wrong trail!" I blurted out. "There's more to it than that! Really there is!"

She shook her head. "Ash, you - you're treating this just as if you're going to do another PCT. I remember all the planning that went into that thing, with all the sacrifices, and now - well, now you're doing it all over again!" She was almost in tears.

"I don't deny that," I responded.

"Bu - but why?!" Her watery eyes were yearning for understanding.

"Because once you start, you can never leave."

She stopped. "What's THAT supposed to mean?"

"Oh, sorry. That's not what I meant to say."

"Then what DID you mean to say?" she demanded.

"Well, simply put," I started, "I know there's a better trail out there than the one I'm presently on."

Pro Verbs knew that, too. But by the look on her face, I could tell that our conversation was over.

On June 1st, 1983, while searching for one of the buildings I had found in the confines of the Yellow Pages, I heard a voice.

The radio was off, and I was traveling alone in my old beat-up Subaru. *Huh?*

"Go to the banner."

The voice - inside my head. Like in that Trailguide –

I didn't know what the statement meant. All I know is that out of nowhere there appeared a banner on the side of the "Church In The Wildwood," above the front door, when I pulled into the main parking lot.

The banner spoke of a special meeting that night in the building.

Oh, good night, I thought. *Time to move on. I hate meetings, and I certainly don't need this stupid banner!*

I pulled my car out of the lot to go type some more plans...

The typewriter was not performing very well, and I began to get frustrated. Time and time again, I inserted a clean sheet of paper through the roller of the machine, and time and time again I typed mistake after mistake.

The pile of crumpled paper was getting as high as the desk. It was composed of many mistakes. The only wastebasket in the room was also overflowing.

"Go to the banner."

Wha - ? I ran to the front door. Yanking it open, I discovered no one there. Fear and panic began to engulf me. "What do you want?!" I yelled, out loud.

"GO TO THE BANNER," I heard again.

I looked down, heart beating wildly. Had I looked up, I might have fainted. Eventually though, I made my way back to the typewriter, but in the process I found myself being consumed by those four words. I could not type anymore.

So I went to the banner.

In the meeting, we opened the Trailguide. The leader of the session, who had been hiking the Trail for quite some time, began to explain how we should interpret the Book Itself.

"Being a lifelong trail," he began, "you must read and digest this Trailguide slowly. Only when you understand the sense of what you are reading do you begin to walk the Trail."

My ears were intent, hanging on every word (although I didn't know exactly why).

"We must now ask the Author of the Trailguide to help us understand what we are about to read. For without His help, this Book will be useless."

Wha – is – here? I stated in my mind.

Going around the room, different ones began to speak to the air, as if the Author was indeed present. There was a long pause after each person finished speaking, and I sensed within each pause that it was my turn to speak.

No! I shouted in my mind. *I don't speak to the air - except - in - private! And I don't even know these people! And I don't even know YOU! And I don't know - if I'm ready to do this - Thing yet!*

But try as I might, I could not escape that sense to arise, and 'speak to the air.'

I stood on shaking knees. Opening my mouth, and speaking somewhat nervously to the air, I don't remember what I said. I only remember sitting down very quickly, breathing a sigh of relief that this moment was behind me.

"Heavenly Father, we - ," spoke the next person to the air. And it was at that moment that it happened. A tidal wave formed in my gut, and culminated inside my head.

'Go to the banner' did not come to me this time, but I knew, regardless.

The God of the PCT had spoken.

"How'd it go?"

I had just arrived back home from the meeting. It was late, and Pro Verbs had waited up for me.

"I talked to Him," I matter-of-factly said. "Then He talked to me. It was nice."

"He - Who - WHAT?" she asked.

"Him," I repeated. "But He also told me that we can't sleep together anymore, since we're not married."

Silence poured thickly into the room. Yet strangely, a sense of peace surrounded me. "What else?" she finally asked.

"Well, no more alcohol and marijuana," I continued. "And I need to start studying this Book," I said, holding up the little bible from the PCT. "It may mean school."

After what seemed like an eternity, Pro Verbs then asked, "So is THIS your new trail?"

I paused, for effect. "What do you think?"

That night, I slept in the spare bedroom amidst former PCT materials. This "Trail" was finally beginning to make sense to me.

For I was finally going home.

I began to walk the Trail the very next day by moving out.

"Ash," Pro Verbs began, in a subsequent letter, "there's no way I can mail you supplies for this Trail. I really can't be a part of it. I wish I could understand what you are doing. So good-bye, and good luck."

I turned to stare out the window of the small travel trailer that was my temporary domicile, courtesy of a local church. "God," I started, "help me. I don't know how to walk this

Trail. I can't even see it. Please help me to walk it the right way. I - I'd like to finish this one, too."

***

Years have passed since the start of this new Trail.

When I hiked the Pacific Crest Trail in 1981, it was in actuality a natural or material footpath that in time led to a spiritual one (I did not know this in 1981).

I now walk this spiritual Trail in God's strength, and not my own. He Himself watched me all through the PCT, and is even now challenging me to a Greater Trail. You too can walk this Trail and know its Author in a unique way, for He Himself is the Way, as delineated in the Trailguide. This Trail, in other words, is a walking relationship with the God of the PCT. You need no heavy gear for this Trail, for His load is easy and His burden is light. You need not be physically strong or a genius in order to walk this Trail, for He will take you as you are, and will give you the strength to walk It. Just come with a willingness to walk with Him as the Trailguide, and He will take you Home.

Believe it. Because there's no There like Going Home.

RESOURCES

"FIRST THE NATURAL;
Schaffer, Jeffrey, and others. "The Pacific Crest Trail: Volumes 1 and 2." Berkeley, CA; Wilderness Press, ©1981.

THEN THE SPIRITUAL"
Douglas, David. "Wilderness Sojourn: Notes In The Desert Silence." San Francisco, CA; Harper & Row Publishers, ©1987.

Heschel, Abraham. "The Prophets." Harper & Row Publishers, NY, ©1962.

Maxwell, Arthur. "Your (Trailguide) Bible and You." ©1979.

CPSIA information can be obtained
at www.ICGtesting.com
Printed in the USA
FSHW011724160919